MW00947588

CRIMINAL JUSTICE:
THEORY IN PRACTICE

RAJUB BHOWMIK

ISBN: 9781072174189

DEDICATION

This book is dedicated to those in law enforcement who have altruistically sacrificed their lives in betterment of our society. And to those who have gone beyond the call of duty, often without fanfare or recognition.

ACKNOWLEDGMENTS

Thank you, divine sprit mystery of the universe, for giving me the courage and willpower to do this project.

Thank you, all of my family members and friends, for your unconditional support.

TABLE OF CONTENTS

ABOUT THE AUTHOR

DR. RAJUB BHOWMIK

Dr. Rajub Bhowmik is an Adjunct Assistant Professor of Law, Police Science, and Criminal Justice, in the Department of Law, Police Science and Criminal Justice Administration at John Jay College of Criminal Justice of the City University of New York. He is also an Adjunct Assistant Professor of Psychology, in the Department of Behavior and Social Science at Hostos Community College of the City University of New York (CUNY). Dr. Rajub Bhowmik is an active law enforcement officer, in the Critical Response Command at Counter-Terrorism Bureau of the New York City Police Department (NYPD).

CHAPTER ONE
THE CRIMINAL JUSTICE SYSTEM

Introduction

The United States (US) justice system is not represented by a single agency, but several organizations (Aliverti, & Bosworth, 2017). The criminal justice system is a network of criminal justice agencies at the local, state, and special judicial and federal levels such as military courts and territorial courts (Feeley, 2017). The US federal criminal justice system adjudicates criminal cases on a national level with espionage, treason, and assassination affiliated with high-level government officials. The state criminal justice system adjudicates all other crimes that do not rise to the federal level (Skeem et al., 2015). The US criminal justice system functions efficiently when each of the criminal justice components are interlinked and coordinated together. The central idea is that the offender pays damages and repents for their criminal activity while giving the victims reparations (Konradi, 2017). The three US criminal justice components are law enforcement, courts, and corrections. The US criminal justice system functions in an organized manner in order to implement the law by rehabilitating, deterring, and punishing people who commit criminal acts (Skeem et al., 2015). Later sections in this book include extensive research on the criminal justice system to help one better understand how the criminal justice works. Therefore, one will be able to form a critical opinion about the offender and the US criminal justice system (Zhang & Jiang, 2017).

The Sequence of Events in the US Criminal Justice System

Crime

Crime is defined as an offense that merits a community punishment or condemnation that is commonly followed by a term of imprisonment, a fine, or both. A crime is more than a civil action against an individual. However, punishments for crime may include restitution or compensation. The state prosecutes criminal offenses; however, an individual is required to initiate a civil court action (Aliverti & Bosworth, 2017). An individual has the right to initiate a criminal proceeding, but it is rare. An assault can be deemed both a civil wrong and a criminal offense. The police initiate the criminal assault case, but the victim initiates the civil action to get restitution or compensation (Feeley, 2017).

Prosecution and a Pretrial Hearing

In the criminal justice system, a criminal case is initiated before an actual trial. The defense and the prosecutor submit the required pretrial arguments that include evidence. A pretrial hearing is the part of the criminal justice law that includes preliminary hearings and evidentiary hearings. Preliminary hearings proceed after the submission of a criminal complaint by the prosecutor (Konradi, 2017). Therefore, the outcome of a case hinges on the result of the pretrial hearings and motions (Alivert & Bosworth, 2017). The law sections elaborate on the different kind of pretrial hearings and motions that can occur during a criminal prosecution.

Adjudication

Adjudication is the legal procedure that refers to the settling of the claims and the legal case via the justice or court system. The adjudication, legal ruling, or judgment directly refers to the final pronouncement in a case. The process of an adjudication can also refer to the procedure of insurance validation decrees as well as claims in bankruptcy proceedings among creditors and citizens (Zhang & Jiang, 2017). There are various types of disputes resolved or handled by adjudication and include the disagreement among single parties, private parties, corporations, and individual entities (Skeem et al., 2015).

Sentencing and Appeal

The appeal is a request to the higher court to review and change the decision of a lower court. The prosecution may appeal the sentence and the defense may appeal the conviction (Hetey & Eberhardt, 2018). A prosecutor may appeal the sentence if they believe the judge acted improperly in handing down the sentence and a higher or decreased sentence is more appropriate. This type of appeal may be requested if the judge's original sentence and the sentencing discretion in similar cases for other offenses are grossly disproportionate (Aliverti & Bosworth, 2017). There are specific time limits for lodging appeals and a US court or magistrate must occur within 28 days from the day of the sentence. The exact time duration is implemented to the appeals interlinked with the US court and the Supreme Court appeal (Reiman & Leighton, 2015).

Prison/Corrections

Prison is as a correctional jail facility, detention center, penitentiary, or internment facility. A prison is the facility in which the state forcibly detains an individual or where inmates are confined or denied freedom as per the state's authority. Most commonly, prison is implemented in the criminal justice system for people who have committed a crime, are charged, and possibly imprisoned until their trial (Cross & Whitcomb, 2017). People who are found guilty or plead guilty to a crime at trial receive a sentence for a specific amount of time. Prison is the basic tool of political repression by authoritarian regimes. Perceived opponents are sometimes imprisoned because of political crimes without due legal process or trial. The majority of public international laws support the civil justice administration (Hamilton, 2016).

The Process of Bringing Crime to the Attention of Police

The process by which the police give attention of the police to a crime is criminal justice. Agencies initiate processes established by state governments to control crime and implement penalties for people that violate the law (Aliverti & Bosworth, 2017). However, there are various individual and combined systems within the criminal justice system. In order for a criminal justice system to function in a specific area, jurisdiction is appointed by the state, city, tribal, federal, or military jurisdiction (Throup, 2017). The laws are established by various jurisdictions while law enforcement agencies manage the criminal justice process (Fattah, 2016). If a person receives a sentence for a crime, they could go to prison. In the state criminal justice system, the specific crimes committed are adjudicated within state boundaries. The federal criminal justice system includes crimes committed on federal property or involving multiple states (Wall, 2015).

The process of criminal justice includes evaluating a specific sequence of events with the jurisdictional boundaries initiated, observed, or reported. The process depends on how the jurisdictional agencies evaluates the complexity of the crime and deem the crime a misdemeanor or felony (Simon, 2017). The accused criminal may be a juvenile or an adult. All crimes committed do not go through the criminal justice system because some crimes are never reported, the inability to identify a suspect, and a lack of evidence (Throup, 2017). The criminal justice process requires several steps with the first being the report. In the report stage, law enforcement attains the required criminal report detailing the sequence of events. The crime report is obtained from witnesses, victims, or other parties involved in the case. The second step is the implementation of law enforcement to investigate the alleged crime (Wall, 2015). Law enforcement investigates the criminal suspect and evaluates the available evidence in order to build a case and arrest the suspect. The third step is the issuance of a citation or an arrest if based on the law, the suspect committed the offense, there is evidence, and the statute of limitations has not expired (Ashworth, 2015). The court's decision relies on the criminal nature of the event and other contributing factors. For example, if the law enforcement officers are unable to identify a suspect or the necessary evidence is insufficient, the criminal case will remain open (Simon, 2017). There are five major law enforcement components in the criminal justice system: 1) law enforcement, 2) the defense attorney, 3) the prosecutor, 4) corrections, and 5) the court. These five components play a significant part in the criminal justice process (Throup, 2017). The prosecutor takes the evidence provided by law enforcement and files formal charges or releases the accused. The criminal justice system, in some cases, becomes intimidating, overwhelming, and confusing when cases do not conclude in a reasonable amount of time (Fattah, 2016).

Production Process Model

The production process model is comprised of three factors such as the police, the courts, and corrections.

Figure 1

Production Process Model (Lynch, 2014)

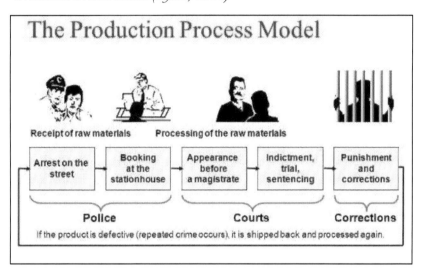

The Production Process Model in terms of criminal prosecutions is comprised of a series of stages that begins with the arrest on the street and ends with punishment and the corrections (Cole et al., 2018). When a criminal defendant accepts a plea bargain offered by the prosecution, the process ends because the defendant accepts a guilty plea before the criminal trial concludes (Leiber & Peck, 2015). The first step in the production process model is the arrest on the street. The criminal prosecution also begins with the arrest. The police officer arrests a person when the officer has probable cause that the person involved has committed the crime (Surette, 2014). The officer is able to complete the arrest by using a valid arrest warrant or probable cause on scene. After completing the arrest, the police place the suspect into custody to book at the stationhouse. If the suspect is involved in a minor crime, the police have the option to issue the suspect a citation instructing them to appear at court later on a specified date (Vera & Fabian, 2016).

Law Enforcement

The initial law enforcement officers involved generate the report for the crime that occurred in their geographical area. Local investigators then respond to the crime scene and collect, and safeguard any evidence. After law enforcement has enough evidence to establish probable cause, the suspect is placed under arrest. Next, law enforcement provides testimony in court and ultimately completes a follow up investigation if needed (Crawford & Evans, 2017).

Prosecution

The prosecutors are the lawyers representing the federal or state government or the victim for the duration of the court proceeding. The prosecutors analyze the evidence provided by law enforcement to decide whether to pursue criminal charges or drop the case (Nelson, 2017). The prosecutors then present the evidence in court, question witnesses, and negotiate with defendants as a means of accomplishing plea bargains (Vogler, 2017). Prosecutors are given immense freedom and discretion in deciding which cases to prosecute. In some cases, victims may provide prosecutors with critical details in order to help with investigating a case (Feeley, 2017).

Defense Attorneys

The defense attorneys represent the accused against the government. The defense attorneys are hired by the defendant or appointed by the court if the defendant is unable to afford an attorney. The prosecutor represents the state, while the defense attorney represents the accused (Surette, 2014).

Courts

The judge operates within the court with their principal role is to decide the case. The court makes the final decision of whether to release the defendant before trial, reject or accept plea bargaining agreements, convict offenders, and overseas the trial (King & Murphy, 2014).

Corrections

The correction officers are involved in the supervision of the convicted offenders subjected to jail, released on parole, or on probation. A process in corrections is important in law enforcement because of the presentencing reports provided that include extensive background information about the offenders in order to assist judges in finalizing sentences (Lynch, 2014). Correction officers provide for the safety and security of the offenders during custody. Correction officers also provide victims with changes in the status of an offender (Wesson, 2016).

The Wedding Cake Model

Samuel Walker developed a theory of the criminal justice process to analyze the judicial system known as the wedding cake model. The criminal justice system is divided into four categories: celebrated cases, serious felonies, less serious felonies, and misdemeanors. A closer analysis of the criminal justice system is provided through the four categories of this theory (Lynch, 2014).

Figure 2

The Wedding Cake Model (Surette, 2014)

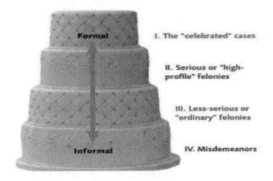

Celebrated Cases

The top layer of the cake is comprised of celebrated cases. These types of cases receive enormous attention from the media because the defendants are high-ranking officials, celebrities, or because the unusual nature of the crime (Cole et al., 2018). High-profile cases are very different from typical criminal cases because these cases usually include cameras in the courtroom and sometimes require crowd control in and around the courtroom. Celebrated cases do not represent the typical operation of the criminal justice system. Celebrated cases are real but are not the norm (Surette, 2014). Examples of celebrated cases include the cases against Michael Jackson, OJ Simpson, and Bernie Madoff (Surette, 2014).

Serious Felonies

The second layer of the cake is serious felonies without the same external factors affecting the system because celebrated cases are not present (Lynch, 2014). These cases include defendants who have committed severe crimes and are not likely to be released on bail. Chances are limited for the defendant to enter into a plea agreement before trial (Surette, 2014).

Lesser Felonies

In the third layer of the cake are the less severe felonies. These types of crimes tend to be non-violent. This group includes crimes such as financial crimes or drug-related charges. A majority of these cases end in plea agreements (Vogler, 2017).

Misdemeanors

The final layer includes the least severe crimes, excluding traffic infractions. The crimes included within this layer are minor thefts and disturbing the peace. Misdemeanors represent the largest category of cases in the criminal justice system and the vast majority of these cases are resolved through plea agreements (Feeley, 2017).

Significance

Using the wedding cake model assists with understanding the operations of the criminal justice system. Understanding the mechanics of the judiciary system occur through the lens of this model. Distinctions made amongst the four categories of cases, particularly between normal criminal proceedings and the celebrated cases, people can better understand the differences between the exceptions and the norms of the criminal justice system (Lynch, 2014).

The Funnel Effect of the Criminal Justice System

The process that involves a series of steps that begins with an investigation about a criminal act and ends with the release of the offender from correctional supervision. The center of the process revolves around decision making and rules (Harris et al., 2017).

Rules

The Bill of Rights, the US Constitution, the US codes, state constitutions, court decisions, state codes, federal rules for criminal procedure, agency rules, department regulations, and state rules for criminal procedures are the sources for the rules in US criminal justice system. The federal rules include governance of the procedures used in the proceedings of criminal cases in United States courts (Zane et al., 2016).

Discretion

In the criminal justice system, decision making involves the knowledge and application of specific rules for certain cases. Discretion is employed in the process of decision making and the judgment of certain choices involves individual exercises to make alternative choices for the best course of action. However, discretion does not have any formal set of rules for decision making in the criminal justice system (Harris et al., 2017). Discretion plays a role in the choices of the police in the investigation, search, arrest, and questioning. Meanwhile, the charges an offender faces and the plea agreements could decrease because prosecutors exercise discretion based on their individual judgment. Discretion is also used by judges to set bail, reject or accept plea agreements, sentencing, and pretrial motion rulings. The release of inmates is decided at the discretion of the parole board members (Zane et al., 2016).

Steps in the Criminal Justice Process

The steps in the criminal justice process begin with the investigation conducted by the police. After the investigation, police gather evidence in preparation for an arrest of a suspect. A search may be required for investigating property or contents on a person. Standards are set for the probable cause required for a search and the facts indicate specific places or persons to search for evidence of criminality (Martínez et al., 2018). This helps make sure the police arrest the right suspect and present them to the court. The legal requirements consist of the probable cause for the arrest with reasonable links between the particular crime and specific person (Zane et al., 2016).

For a prosecution by a district attorney of a criminal defendant to be successful it is mandatory for the prosecutor to get as much knowledge about the particular crime committed and the suspect charged (Harris et al. 2017). The filing of an indictment by a prosecutor through a grand jury is critical. An indictment is given to a prosecutor and information about imprisonment regarding a crime is provided (Martínez, Slack, & Martínez-Schuldt, 2018).

Using standards help with getting an indication of the probable cause required for the filing of charges from the prosecutor's files. The attorney for the defendant is present to hear disputes related to the charges. Defendants appear before the court at arraignment in front of a judge. A plea is entered by the defendant as guilty or not guilty (Clear, 2018). The temporary custody of a defendant is referred to as pretrial detention if bail is not met. Bail is the amount paid by the defendant to ensure the court that the defendant will attend trial. Plea bargaining occurs between the prosecutor and defense attorney and is the exchange of sentence reduction or charge reduction for the defendant (Braga et al., 2014). The judge analyzes the defense attorney and prosecutor's participation in the adjudication of guilt. Trials are held with the assistance of a jury or judge. During trial doubts and reasons are justified for further supervision (Clear, 2018).

Guilt is assessed in the sentencing by the judge and may include probation, a fine, a period of incarceration, community service, or supervised release. Defendants require the appellate judge's rule in the appellate court when a defense attorney appeals the original decision (Zane et al., 2016). If an appeal is granted, a retrial occurs in court. The prosecutor then must decide to either retry the case or drop the charges (Harris et al. 2017). The statute of limitations must be considered when deciding whether to prosecute the defendant for the accused crime. Statues are imposed to limit the amount of time the government is able to bring charges against a defendant. After a case is complete, the terms on rehabilitation and/or punishment are applied (Braga et al., 2014).

Discretion: Police

Legislators, leaders, and commentators commonly use the term discretion. Using discretion helps police officers with the way they act when stopping and arresting people. Discretion ensures flexibility and satisfaction. Discretion could lead to inequity by the police (Schulenberg, 2015). Discretion is termed as the ability and power of decision making. Generally, it is the concept termed in the context of policing. Some leeway is provided to police officers to understand the impact of choices of the people they are policing

(Nowacki, 2015). Some police departments exercise more discretion than others do because of the capability of attaining desired goals while maintaining the safety of the people. Conversely, some police departments do not exercise enough discretion, as officers are not successfully able to attain goals and maintain the safety of the people (Schulenberg, 2015). Policing is one of the central areas where discretion is applied because investigatory stops are driven by discretion. Each police department is different and each police department exerts a different level of discretion based on a particular situation (Ariel et al. 2016).

Discretion: Prosecution

Prosecuting attorneys have nearly unreviewable and absolute power when deciding whether to bring charges against a defendant, commonly referred to as prosecutorial discretion. Prosecuting attorneys decide if charges are justified by the evidence (Price, 2014). This authority provides the required underpinnings to the practice of plea bargaining and in turn provides prosecutors the title of the most powerful public officials. Significant opportunities for mercy and leniency are provided in a system marked by both harsh and broad criminal laws and have increased in the 20th century for sentencing discretion on judges by legislative limitation (Cass, 2015).

American law is ingrained deeply with the broad discretion often assumed by inevitable prosecutorial discretion. In contrast, some European countries adhere to opposite standards with mandates that the prosecution charge defendants if it is supported by the evidence presented by the citizens or the police (McConville et al., 2017). The extent in which this practice is actually followed in these countries is controversial. Mainly, some scholars believed the discretion exercised by US prosecutors is comparable to the discretion exercised by the police in these European countries (Price, 2014).

Discretion: Judge

Some discretionary legal decisions made by the judicial system are judicial discretion. This discretion is based on the ability of judges to act with judicial independence and under the separation of power under doctrine. The range of possible decisions available to judges with the use of judicial discretion depends on the legal case (McConville et al., 2017). If the discretion goes beyond the established set of constraints formed by legislation, the court may be abusing discretion and undermining the rule of law. This may result in the court using judicial activism to make decisions (Price, 2014).

Judicial power as contradistinguished from the power of the law has no existence. Courts are mere instruments of the law and even mere legal discretion is discerning the course of the law because it is the duty of the court to follow the law. In respect to recidivism and other similar issues, mandatory sentencing, sex offender's registry laws, and three strikes laws have been introduced in the US. These examples represent the limitations of judicial discretion in sentencing (McConville et al., 2017).

Discretion: Parole Board

The court ultimately decides whether murderers and other offenders return into the community or not. Notorious prisoners released early feel opprobrium from members of the public and press. Because of opprobrium, the parole board's decision can be one of life or death (Spohn, 2018). There are many cases where violent criminals have harmed ordinary people in the community. Therefore, it is essential to keep violent criminals in custody to manage the safety of the community. The criminal justice system grants enormous power to the parole board and assists judges with oral hearings in high-profile cases, which the judge considers when the sentence is indeterminate (Cass, 2015). These offenders usually remain in jail regardless of feeling guilty for the acts committed. Violent and sexual offenses are the crimes that cause harm and risk to society; however, after serving the minimum sentence, the offender could return to society (Spohn, 2018). Determinate and indeterminate prison sentences are considered regarding each prisoner. Panels commence in order to discuss pending issues and make decisions. Assessing parole situations could take several weeks. Deliberation panels sit down to create reports and record all decisions before the criminal is released. Furthermore, members are identified to speak their opinions freely about the case (McConville et al., 2017).

Chapter Summary

In conclusion, the US criminal justice system is an all-encompassing organization. The criminal justice system is a network of criminal justice agencies at the state, and special judicial and federal levels, which include military courts and territorial courts. The US criminal justice system is one in which all the laws are dependent on the US constitution. The US federal justice criminal system regulates criminal cases nationally and includes charges such as espionage, treason, and the assassination of high-level government officials. Crime is defined as an offense that merits a community punishment and condemnation commonly followed by a term of imprisonment or a fine. The process by which the attention of the police is given to crime is referred to as criminal justice. Local agencies follow procedures established by the state government in order to control crime and implement the penalties for people who violate the laws. The criminal justice system, in some cases, becomes intimidating, overwhelming, and confusing if it is not initiated in a timely manner. The process ends when the criminal defendant agrees to a bargained plea offered by the prosecution or convicted in a criminal trial. Generally, in terms of the plea bargain agreement, the defendant selects a guilty plea before a trial commences.

References

Aliverti, A., & Bosworth, M. (2017). Introduction: Criminal Justice Adjudication in an Age of Migration. New Criminal Law Review: In International and Interdisciplinary Journal, 20(1), 1-11.

Ariel, B., Sutherland, A., Henstock, D., Young, J., Drover, P., Sykes, J., & Henderson, R. (2016). Report: increases in police use of force in the presence of body-worn cameras are driven by officer discretion: a protocol-based subgroup analysis of ten randomized experiments. Journal of Experimental Criminology, 12(3), 453-463.

Ashworth, A. (2015). Sentencing and criminal justice. Cambridge University Press.

Braga, A. A., Papachristos, A. V., & Hureau, D. M. (2014). The effects of hot spots policing on crime: An updated systematic review and meta-analysis. Justice quarterly, 31(4), 633-663.

Cass, R. A. (2015). Power Failures: Prosecution, Discretion, and the Demise of Official Constraint (No. 05-2015). ICER-International Centre for Economic Research.

Clear, T. R. (2018). The community justice ideal. Routledge.

Cole, G. F., Smith, C. E., & DeJong, C. (2018). The American system of criminal justice. Cengage Learning.

Crawford, A., & Evans, K. (2017). Crime prevention and community safety (pp. 797-824). Oxford University Press.

Cross, T. P., & Whitcomb, D. (2017). The practice of prosecuting child maltreatment: Results of an online survey of prosecutors. Child abuse & neglect, 69, 20-28.

Dolovich, S., &Natapoff, A. (Eds.). (2017). The New Criminal Justice Thinking. NYU Press.

Fattah, E. A. (Ed.). (2016). From crime policy to victim policy: Reorienting the justice system. Springer.

Feeley, M. (2017). Two models of the criminal justice system: An organizational perspective. In Crime, Law and Society (pp. 119-137). Routledge.

Hamilton, R. (2016, January). Adjudicating the State's Role in International Crime. In Proceedings of the ASIL Annual Meeting (Vol. 110, pp. 156-160). Cambridge University Press.

Harris, A., Huebner, B., Martin, K., Pattillo, M., Pettit, B., Shannon, S., & Fernandes, A. (2017). Monetary Sanctions in the Criminal Justice System.

Hetey, R. C., & Eberhardt, J. L. (2018). The numbers don't speak for themselves: Racial disparities and the persistence of inequality in the criminal justice system. Current Directions in Psychological Science, 27(3), 183-187.

King, C., & Murphy, G. H. (2014). A systematic review of people with autism spectrum disorder and the criminal justice system. Journal of autism and developmental disorders, 44(11), 2717-2733.

Konradi, A. (2017). Can justice be served on campus? An examination of due process and victim protection policies in the campus adjudication of sexual assault in Maryland. Humanity & Society, 41(3), 373-404.

Leiber, M. J., & Peck, J. H. (2015). Race, gender, crime severity, and decision making in the juvenile justice system. Crime & Delinquency, 61(6), 771-797.

Lynch, G. E. (2014). Our administrative system of criminal justice. Fordham L. Rev., 83, 1673.

Martínez, D. E., Slack, J., & Martínez-Schuldt, R. (2018). The Rise of Mass Deportation in the United States. The Handbook of Race, Ethnicity, Crime, and Justice, 173-201.

McConville, M., Sanders, A., & Leng, R. (2017). Routledge Revivals: Case for the Prosecution (1991): Police Suspects and the Construction of Criminality. Routledge.

Nelson, F. M. (2017). Indonesian pretrial: Can it fulfil the rights of the victims of an unfair trial to restoration? In Law and Justice in a Globalized World (pp. 51-56). Routledge.

Nowacki, J. S. (2015). Organizational-level police discretion: An application for police use of lethal force. Crime & delinquency, 61(5), 643-668.

Price, Z. S. (2014). Enforcement discretion and executive duty. Vand. L. Rev., 67, 671.

Reiman, J., & Leighton, P. (2015). Rich Get Richer and the Poor Get Prison, The (Subscription): Ideology, Class, and Criminal Justice. Routledge.

Schulenberg, J. L. (2015). Moving beyond arrest and conceptualizing police discretion: An investigation into the factors affecting conversation, assistance, and criminal charges. Police Quarterly, 18(3), 244-271.

THEORIES AND PRACTICES IN CRIMINAL JUSTICE

Simon, J. (2017). Governing through crime. In Law and Poverty (pp. 97-115). Routledge.

Skeem, J. L., Steadman, H. J., & Manchak, S. M. (2015). Applicability of the risk-need-responsivity model to persons with mental illness involved in the criminal justice system. Psychiatric services, 66(9), 916-922.

Spohn, C. (2018). Reflections on the exercise of prosecutorial discretion 50 years after publication of The Challenge of Crime in a Free Society. Criminology & Public Policy, 17(2), 321-340.

Surette, R. (2014). Media, crime, and criminal justice. Nelson Education.

Throup, D. (2017). Crime, politics and the police in colonial Kenya, 1939–63. In Policing and decolonization. Manchester University Press.

Vera, Y., & Fabian, N. (2016). Crime prevention through environmental design.

Vogler, R. (2017). A world view of criminal justice. Routledge.

Wall, D. S. (2015). The Internet as a conduit for criminal activity.

Wesson, M. (2016). The Chow: Depictions of the Criminal Justice System as a Character in Crime Fiction. New Eng. L. Rev., 51, 263.

Zane, S. N., Welsh, B. C., & Drakulich, K. M. (2016). Assessing the impact of race on the juvenile waiver decision: A systematic review and meta-analysis. Journal of Criminal Justice, 46, 106-117.

Zhang, C., & Jiang, M. (2017, November). An explanation of the sentencing of willful and malicious injury crime based on inference rules. In Intelligent Systems and Knowledge Engineering (ISKE), 2017 12th International Conference on (pp. 1-4). IEEE.

CHAPTER TWO
LEGAL ISSUES FOR THE POLICE

Introduction

Police in Clevland, Ohio found pistols in the possession of Richard Chilton and John Terry. The two men were tried and convicted of carrying concealed weapons. The two men appealed the decision arguing for the exclusion of the evidence based on an unconstitutional frisk. The decision was later affirmed by the Ohio Supreme Court. The temporary detention of a person in order to conduct an investigation is known as stop and occurs when the police assert their authority and restrict an individual's movement. This case confirmed that a stop did occur. A limited search of a person's outer clothing is known as frisk and is conducted in order to discover concealed weapons or dangerous instruments. The Fourth Amendment restricts law enforcement agencies from conducting unreasonable searches and safeguards private citizens against unannounced and unreasonable searches and seizures. The Supreme Court decision stemmed from the stop being constitutional; therefore, the evidence could be used in the criminal prosecution. There are several different cases involving the legal issues and applications of the fourth amendment. In some cases, the search was deemed legal and in other cases deemed illegal. An analysis of these cases has been conducted in order to present a

41

better understanding about the courts decisions as it pertains to the protections provided to citizens by the Fourth Amendment.

Description of the Fourth Amendment

The Fourth Amendment is about securing the rights of people in their homes, persons, effects, and papers against unreasonable searches and seizures. Furthermore, the Fourth Amendment states the probable cause standard must be met for the issuance of warrants and reinforced by affirmation or oath to describe the specific place to search and the specific things or persons to be seized. As with other US laws, this amendment was drawn from old colonial English legal doctrine (Hanlon, 2015). The development of the Fourth Amendment occurred to limit the power of government intrusion as well as to protect the rights of the people. The creation of the Fourth Amendment resulted from the abuse of the writs of assistance during the American Revolution. The Fourth Amendment is one of the ten Amendments included in the Bills of Rights of the US Constitution (Kerr, 2016).

What is a Terry Stop?

The term Terry Stop, also known as a Stop, Question and Frisk, emerged from the U.S. Supreme Court case, Terry v. Ohio. A Terry Stop is a seizure as described in the Fourth Amendment. A Terry Stop is more accurately defined as the brief detention of a suspect by a police officer whom the officer reasonably suspects has committed or is about to commit, or is committing a crime.

Similarly, "a vehicle stop follows the same rules as a Terry Stop when the police detain the occupants of a vehicle involved in a traffic violation" (Nowak & Glenn, 2017, p. 16-29).

What is a Frisk?

When the police stop an individual they reasonably suspect has committed, is about to commit, or is committing a crime, the officer may frisk the suspect for weapons. A frisk is a pat-down of the suspect's outer clothing to search for weapons. Although the Fourth Amendment protects the rights of individuals against unreasonable searches and seizures, the Supreme Court ruled in Terry v. Ohio that the stop and frisk of those suspects was reasonable (Meares, 2015, p. 159).

What is Probable Cause?

US criminal law requires the police to meet the probable cause standard prior to arresting a suspect or seizing property. Probable cause originated from the Fourth Amendment and ensures that an individual's rights are not violated. "Search warrants and arrest warrants cannot be issued if probable cause does not exist" (Goel et al., 2016, p. 365-394). Arrest warrants and search warrants are issued by the courts. In some cases, the police may conduct an arrest without a warrant if probable cause exists. Prosecutors cannot charge a defendant if probable cause does not exist. Probable cause must be present for the issuance of warrants, in making summary arrests, in conducting searches, and for seizing property. "A judge must agree that probable cause exists to ensure any unreasonable action in contrast with the Fourth Amendment is avoided" (Saunders et al., 2016, p. 92-98).

What is Reasonable Suspicion?

Reasonable suspicion is a legal standard of proof and less than probable cause, but more than a hunch. "The use of reasonable suspicion must be based on specific and articulable facts and the suspicion must be associated with a specific individual" (Saunders et al., 2016, p. 92-98). The police can frisk a person for weapons if the police have reasonable suspicion that the person is armed and dangerous; however, the person cannot be frisked for contraband like drugs. Reasonable suspicion is evaluated using the reasonable person or reasonable officer standard. "The use of reasonable suspicion depends on the totality of circumstances and based on the combination of multiple facts to form the justification" (Goel et al., 2016, p. 365-394).

Rights of Search and Seizure

Constitutional rights under the Fourth Amendment protect individuals from unlawful searches or seizures. A seizure occurs when a government agent or employee intrudes on a person's privacy. During a seizure of a person, the specific circumstances of the encounter are reviewed, and if warranted, the person is not allowed to leave or ignore the police. "The seizure of property occurs if a meaningful interference of an individual's property is infringed upon" (Saunders et al., 2016, p. 92-98).

Terry V. Ohio

On June 10, 1968, the U.S. Supreme Court issued the decision for Terry v. Ohio. The decision determined that police encounters that are labeled stop and frisks, where members of the public are stopped, questioned, and patted down for drugs and weapons without the legal standard of probable cause, does not constitute a violation of the Fourth Amendment's prohibition on unreasonable searches and seizures (Nowak & Glenn, 2017). The case involved the actions of a Cleveland police detective, Martin McFadden, who conducted a search in order to prevent a suspected armed robbery. "On October 31, 1963, Detective McFadden conducted a pat-down on three men he believed were preparing to rob a store" (Carbado, 2017, p. 1508).

Two of the men, Richard Chilton and John Terry, were found to be in possession of pistols. The men went to trial and convicted for carrying concealed weapons and appealed the convictions arguing that the evidence gathered was the result of an illegal search. The Ohio Supreme Court affirmed the convictions and in 1967, the U.S. Supreme Court heard Terry's case. Chief Justice Earl Warren ruled in the majority opinion that is was permissible for McFadden to conduct a pat down for his safety. "This type of pat-down did constitute a search according to the Fourth Amendment, however, Chief Justice Warren determined that such a stop and frisk did not

45

violate the ban on unreasonable searches and seizures" (Davies, 2017, pp. 473-475).

The ruling stopped short of creating a new standard for police actions, which did not rise to probable cause. "The courts analysis of whether the search violated the Fourth Amendment prohibiting unreasonable searches and seizures focused on if the actions of the officer at the start of the search were reasonable and whether the actions were consistent during the initial search" (Nowak & Glenn, 2017, p. 16-29). The Court rejected the argument that a pat down is a petty indignity for the individual searched. "The Court also noted the potential detrimental impact stop and frisks may have on police-community relationships; however, at the time the officer suspected the person of being armed, it was reasonable for the officer to perform the search in order to protect the officer and others from danger" (Carbado, 2017, p. 1508).

William Douglas was the lone dissenter in the case and he claimed the Court was now providing more legal authority to the police for conducting searches and seizures on the street than justices have in authorizing a court order for a search or seizure. Justice Douglas further argued that searches by the police must be constrained to the probable cause standard. Justice Douglas was worried that providing police with more authority and power could be at the expense of the individual's liberty (Davies, 2017, p. 473-475).

Stop and Frisks

Stops

The temporary detention of a person in order to conduct an investigation is a stop. A stop occurs when the police assert their authority and restrict an individual's movements and actions. During a stop, the person is under the reasonable impression to not move, to not ignore the officer, or leave the scene without permission (Saunders et al., 2016).

Procedure

The following sections: identification, duration, explanation, rights, refusals, and uses of force contain information on the legal procedures of a stop.

Identification

An officer must identify himself or herself as law enforcement and if they are not in uniform, they must display their badge or identification.

Duration of a Stop

A person may be detained on scene for a reasonable amount of time. The officer may only detain a person for an amount of time necessary to verify the person's conduct, presence, accounts of events, and suspected offenses. After the reasonable detainment period, the officer must release or arrest the person (Meares, 2015).

Explanation to the Detained Person

The officer towards the person may use courtesy while they are stopped. The officer must provide an explanation of the stop.

Rights of the Detained Person

The officer may ask direct questions to the person detained such as their address, name, and explanation of conduct. The person does not have to produce identification or to answer any questions, although the officer can make these requests. "The operator of a motor vehicle is required to produce a valid driver's license upon request during a lawful traffic stop" (Goel et al., 2016, p. 365-394).

Effects of Refusing to Cooperate

Not providing identification and refusing to cooperate, coupled with the totality of the circumstances, could result in an arrest or other police action.

Use of Force

The officer may use a reasonable amount of force during a lawful stop. "An officer may use the level of force necessary to place an individual into custody" (Saunders et al., 2016, p. 92-98).

Frisks

A frisk is a limited protective search with the sole purpose of finding concealed weapons or dangerous instruments. A frisk is not performed to recover evidence such as drugs or property.

Procedure

An officer performs a frisk by patting down an individual stopped only when the officer reasonably believes the person is armed and dangerous with a concealed weapon. The outer clothing of the person stopped may be felt by the officer in order to determine if a weapon is present. If the outer clothing is too bulky, an officer may check the inner clothing (Goel et al., 2016). If the officer detects an object during the frisk and believe it is a weapon, the officer can search that area and retrieve the weapon.

Vehicle Stops

During a vehicle stop, if the officer believes that a weapon or dangerous instrument is present inside a vehicle, the officer may examine the inside of the vehicle. A frisk may be extended to the passengers or driver of a vehicle if it is determined that one of the occupants has a weapon or dangerous instrumentd.

Containers

If the officer reasonably believes a dangerous instrument or weapon is present inside a container, the officer can examine and look inside to determine the contents.

49

Use of Force

An officer may justifiably use the necessary amount of force to defend himself or herself from an attack by a person or in order to make a lawful arrest (Meares, 2015).

The Fourth Amendment and the Exclusionary Rule

The Fourth Amendment was ratified in 1791 and became a part of the US Constitution in 1792. The Fourth Amendment was of little use to defendants during criminal prosecutions because even when evidence obtained by the police in violation of a warrant and reasonable requirements, the evidence was admissible in court. In 1914, the Supreme Court dramatically changed the jurisprudence of the Fourth Amendment after handing down the Weeks v. United States decision. The defendant in the case was convicted based on evidence seized by a federal agent without constitutional justification or a warrant. The defendant's conviction was reversed and the exclusionary rule created. "In 1961, the Supreme Court applied the exclusionary rule to the states in Mapp v. Ohio" (Kerr, 2016, p. 1117).

The purpose of the exclusionary rule is to minimize misconduct by the police by suppressing incriminating evidence at trial if the evidence obtained was done so in violation of the constitution. The exclusionary rule permits the defense to challenge the admissibility of evidence during a pretrial motion and if the evidence is found to be obtained unconstitutionally, the evidence is suppressed. The defendant is allowed to appeal and challenge the accuracy of the trial court's decision to deny a motion to suppress if a jury decides to convict the defendant based on evidence introduced to the court (Walsh & Sullivan, 2018). The Supreme Court has ruled that double jeopardy does not apply with the exclusionary rule because the trial court's error was not addressing guilt or innocence, but a procedural error. In 1988, the Supreme Court affirmed this opinion in Lockhart v. Nelson (Kerr, 2016).

Case Analysis

Mapp v. Ohio

Mapp v. Ohio is one of the most famous Supreme Court decisions regarding criminal procedures in the US. The Supreme Court declared that the federal government or any US state could not use evidence obtained by the prosecution in violation of the Fourth Amendment or any (Thomas, 2014). The Fourth Amendment restricts law enforcement from conducting unreasonable searches and seizures. This decision declared that evidence obtained unconstitutionally could not be used in criminal prosecutions and became known as the exclusionary rule. The defendant in this case, Dollree Mapp was involved in illegal gambling operations under the protection of organized crime. Her boyfriend, Virgil Ogletree, was wanted for questioning in a bombing incident and was suspected of being inside her house. Police arrived at Mapp's home, but she refused to let them in without a warrant. A few hours later a dozen law enforcement officers returned with a warrant and searched for Ogletree (Lewis,

2016). Not only did the police find Ogletree, they also found other incriminating evidence ranging from betting slips to pornographic materials. Mapp was subsequently arrested and charged with gambling offenses, but the charges were dropped. Several months after the acquittal, Mapp refused to testify against a notorious mobster on trial for attempting to shakedown Don King. Mapp was charged and indicted for the pornographic materials found in her home and found guilty at trial and sentenced to one to seven years in prison (Thomas, 2014). Mapp appealed her conviction to the Ohio Supreme Court, but they affirmed her conviction. Mapp then appealed her case to the Supreme Court, who overturned her conviction and decided the exclusionary rule did not only apply to the federal government but also applied to each US state.

Miranda v. Arizona

The Supreme Court's decision in Miranda v. Arizona addressed issues involving four separate cases on custodial interrogations. In each cases, detectives, cops, or prosecutors questioned the defendant in a room cut off from the outside world (Kamisar, 2017). In none of these cases was the defendant given a full and compelling warning of their rights at the beginning of the interrogation. In each of these cases, the questioning evoked verbal admissions of guilt and in three cases, signed statements were used against the defendants at trial.

Miranda was arrested at home, taken into custody, and transported to the police station where and identified by the complaining witness. Two cops then interrogated him and after two hours, he signed a written confession. At trial, the oral and written confessions were presented to the jury (Maclin, 2015). Miranda was subsequently found guilty of rape and kidnapping and was sentenced to twenty to thirty years on each count. Miranda appealed to the Arizona Supreme Court, which affirmed his conviction and held that Miranda's constitutional rights were not violated when getting his confessions. Miranda then appealed to the US Supreme Court and the conviction was overturned. The Supreme Court held that the Fifth Amendment applies to settings outside of criminal court proceedings and serves to ensure the protection of people in all settings as a means of not implicating themselves in criminal activity (Kamisar, 2017). As a result, defendants should receive warnings, commonly known as the Miranda Warnings prior to any type of custodial interrogation.

United States v. Watson

In 1972, a postal inspector received information from a confidential informant that Henry Watson was in possession of stolen credit cards. This source had supplied reliable information in the past. The source provided the postal inspector with a stolen card. The postal inspector requested that the source set up another meeting with Watson to deliver more stolen credit cards. The informant set up another meeting and police arrested Watson. The officers read Watson his Miranda Warnings but did not recover any stolen credit cards from him. The officers asked Watson for permission to search his vehicle and Watson gave consent. The officers subsequently recovered two stolen credit cards from Watson's vehicle. Watson was charged with four counts of possession of stolen mail. Before trial, Watson motioned to suppress the evidence by arguing that his arrest was illegal because there was no warrant and the search of his vehicle was improper because he was not informed of his right to deny consent. The motion was denied and Watson was indicted and convicted. The US Court of Appeals for the Ninth Circuit overturned his conviction and held that his arrest was unlawful because the postal inspector had adequate time to obtain a warrant yet failed to do so. In addition, The Court of Appeals held that the permission to search his vehicle was forced and subsequently illegal under the Fourth Amendment (United States v. Watson. n.d.). The US Supreme Court heard the case and held that postal inspectors do have the authority to make summary arrests without warrants when probable cause is present, so the arrest was constitutional. Furthermore, because the arrest was constitutional, the search of the vehicle was also constitutional.

Payton v. New York

Theodore Payton was suspected of murdering a New York City gas station manager. The police forcibly entered Payton's home thinking he was inside. Payton was not home at the time, but the police discovered evidence inside his home connecting him to the murder (Walton, 2016). The police did not have a search warrant and acted under a New York law that enabled the police to enter a private residence to make a felony arrest without first obtaining a warrant. The evidence obtained by the police was presented during the trial. Payton was unable to have the evidence suppressed and was convicted. The judge ruled that the police were authorized to enter his residence without a warrant under New York law, concluding that the search was lawful and the evidence was admissible (Payton v. New York, n.d.). Payton appealed his conviction, but the court affirmed the decision.

The Supreme Court overturned the conviction stating that the New York law that permitted warrantless searches and arrests violated the Fourth Amendment. The Supreme Court ruled that the Fourth Amendment, as applied to the states by the Fourteenth Amendment, prohibits the police from making warrantless entries into residences in order to make routine felony arrests. The Court concluded that absent exigent circumstances, an arrest warrant was required to enter a person's residence if police suspect the suspect is inside the home. "The Payton case and related case law established the precedent that a man in his own home is entitled to Fourth Amendment protections" (Walton, 2016, p. 1094).

Chimel v. California

In Chimel v. California (1969), police entered the home of Chimel with an arrest warrant to arrest him for a burglary. The police were invited into Chimel's home by his wife and Chimel was not home, so the police waited for him to return. When Chimel returned home, the police served him with his arrest warrant. After accepting his arrest warrant, Chimel denied the police consent to search his home for evidence. The police proceeded to search Chimel's home without his consent and instructed Chimel's wife to empty drawers and discovered coins and other items presented as evidence during the trial. Chimel unsuccessfully attempted to have the items seized suppressed from evidence and was convicted based largely on the evidence seized from his home. Chimel appealed but his conviction was affirmed. Before the Chimel ruling, the courts allowed the police to search the area within the arrestee's possession and control for evidence. The courts maintained that searches that extended past a person's reachable area were also lawful.

The Supreme Court overturned the conviction and ruled that the search of Chimel's entire home was unconstitutional under the Fourth and Fourteenth Amendments because searches are to be restricted to areas within the arrestee's immediate reachable area. The Supreme Court further explained that the police could only search the area within the immediate control of the arrestee after the arrest and a search beyond that would require a search warrant. The Supreme Court stressed the importance of warrants and probable cause as essential safeguards against governmental abuse (Chimel v. California, n.d.).

Minnesota v. Dickerson

Timothy Dickerson was found in a known drug area. An officer decided to pat Dickerson down for weapons and felt an object in Dickerson's coat and retrieved it. The object was drugs, specifically cocaine. "During trial, Dickerson argued that the cocaine should be suppressed because the officer violated his rights under the Fourth Amendment, which protected him against unreasonable searches and seizures" (Khammanivong et al., 2016, p. 2168-2182). The court disagreed and Dickerson was convicted. The Appeals Court overturned the conviction and the Supreme Court ultimately agreed with the Appeals Court's decision.

The Supreme Court unanimously held that when an officer is conducting a legal pat down for weapons and feels something that he or she believes is contraband, the contraband could be retrieved and seized although it is not a weapon. However, the Supreme Court ruled by a six to three vote that the officer in this case had performed an improper pat down therefore, making the search and the resulting seizure of the contraband unconstitutional under the Fourth Amendment (Minnesota v. Dickerson, n.d.).

Arizona v. Hicks

A bullet was fired through the floor of James Hicks' apartment and struck a man in the apartment below him. The police entered Hicks' apartment searching for the shooter and other possible victims. During the search, an officer came across expensive stereo equipment and suspected it was stolen (Herauf & Kuntz, 2015). The officer obtained the serial numbers and checked to determine if the equipment was stolen. The officer determined that the items were stolen during an armed robbery and seized the items and arrested Hicks for robbery. During the trial, Hicks argued that the evidence should be suppressed as it was a violation of his rights under the Fourth Amendment and the court agreed.

The Supreme Court agreed with the lower court's ruling. The Supreme Court concluded that the search and seizure violated the Fourth and Fourteenth Amendments. Referring to a previous ruling in the Coolidge v. New Hampshire (1971), Justice Scalia upheld that the plain view doctrine, which permits the police to seize evidence under certain circumstances without a warrant. However, since the officer who seized the evidence in Hick's apartment only had reasonable suspicion and not probable cause, the officer was in violation of the Fourth and Fourteenth Amendments (Arizona v. Hicks, n.d.).

California v. Greenwood

The police suspected Billy Greenwood was dealing drugs out of his home. The police did not have enough evidence to obtain a search warrant and decided to search his garbage. After searching the trash, the police were able to obtain enough evidence to obtain a search warrant. The police conducted a search and gathered enough evidence inside the home to bring felony drug charges against Greenwood (Huijser et al., 2016). The trial court dismissed the charges against Greenwood noting the search of Greenwood's garbage violated the Fourth Amendment and the appeals court agreed with the decision.

The Supreme Court reversed the decision by a vote of six to two, stating that a search of garbage left at the curb did not violate the Fourth Amendment. The Court concluded that there was no reasonable expectation of privacy afforded to garbage left at the curb. The Court additionally noted the police could not ignore criminal activity observed by a member of the public (California v. Greenwood, n.d.).

Whren v. United States

Michael Whren and James Brown were driving in a high drug area. Two plainclothes officers from the Vice Squad were patrolling the area in an unmarked vehicle and spotted Whren and Brown sitting in a vehicle for approximately twenty seconds while stopped at a stop sign. As the officers approached the vehicle, the vehicle fled the scene speeding and the driver failed to use a turning signals (Kamisar, 2017). The officers stopped the vehicle for the traffic infractions. When the officers approached the vehicle, the officers saw Wren holding two plastic bags of alleged cocaine and other drugs in plain view. Whren and Brown were arrested and charged with felony drug charges. During the trial, the defendants' attorney argued to suppress the evidence based on a violation of the Fourth Amendment in that the officers only used the traffic violations as a pretext to investigate other crimes. The trial court convicted both men and the appeals court affirmed the convictions.

The Supreme Court's ruling was unanimous. As long as the officers had reasonable suspicion that a traffic infraction had occurred, they were permitted to stop the vehicle and concluded that the officers were not in violation of the search and seizure based on the Fourth Amendment because of the lawful vehicle stop. The personal motivation of the officers was irrelevant as long as the stop was lawful (Whren v. United States, n.d.).

Brewer v. Williams

Robert Williams escaped from a mental hospital and began living at a YMCA in Des Moines, Iowa. Shortly after Williams began living at the YMCA, a ten-year-old girl went missing from the YMCA. "Soon after the little girl disappeared, another kid saw Williams carrying a large package to his car with two skinny white legs hanging out" (Herauf & Kuntz, 2015, p. 79). The following day police discovered Williams' car abandoned about 160 miles away in Davenport, Iowa. Williams turned himself into the Davenport Police Department and the Davenport police arrested him, read him his Miranda warnings, and transported him back to Des Moines. Williams told the officers that he would confess once he spoke with his attorney in Des Moines. During the transport, an officer told Williams that the little girl's family wanted to give her a Christian burial and suggested to go find the little girls' body; therefore, leading the police to the little girls' body. During the trial, Williams argued that all the evidence obtained from the transport conversation should be suppressed as it violated his Sixth Amendment right to counsel. The court disagreed and Williams was convicted of murder yet, the appeals court overturned his conviction.

The Supreme Court agreed with the appeals court, ruling that William's Sixth Amendment right to counsel was violated and that William's did not waive his right to counsel when he led the police to the little girls' body (Brewer v. Williams, n.d.).

Chapter Summary

TThe right of people in their homes, persons, effects, and papers against unreasonable searches and seizures is the basis of The Fourth Amendment. Furthermore, there must be probable cause for the issuance of warrants and reinforced by affirmation or oath as well as describe the specific place to search and the specific things or persons to seize.

The most famous decision the Supreme Court issued was in the Terry v. Ohio case. The Court held that police encounters that are labeled stop and frisks are not a violation of the Fourth Amendment.

Numerous cases have been heard by the Supreme Court involving the application and limitations of the Fourth Amendment. In some cases, the search was deemed legal while in others it was deemed illegal. It is important to understand the rulings of the different court cases that the Supreme Court has heard regarding the Fourth Amendment. These rulings serve to protect the citizens from unreasonable searches and seizures as well as to guide law enforcement as to what is legal and what is illegal.

References

Arizona v. Hicks. (n.d.). Oyez. Retrieved September 12, 2018 from https://www.oyez.org/cases/1986/85-1027.

Brewer v. Williams. (n.d.). Oyez. Retrieved September 12, 2018 from https://www.oyez.org/cases/1976/74-1263.

California v. Greenwood. (n.d.). Oyez. Retrieved September 12, 2018 from https://www.oyez.org/cases/1987/86-684.

Carbado, D. W. (2017). From stop and frisk to shoot and kill: Terry v. Ohio's pathway to police violence. UCLA L. Rev., 64, 1508.

Chimel v. California. (n.d.). Oyez. Retrieved September 12, 2018 from https://www.oyez.org/cases/1968/770.

Davies, T. A. (2017). The Chicago Freedom Movement: Martin Luther King Jr. and Civil Rights Activism in the North. In Mary Lou Finley, Bernard Lafayette Jr., James R. Ralph Jr., and Pam Smith (Eds.). Journal of Southern History, 83(2), 473-475.

Goel, S., Rao, J. M., & Shroff, R. (2016). Precinct or prejudice? Understanding racial disparities in New York City's stop and frisk policy. The Annals of Applied Statistics, 10(1), 365-394.

Hanlon, C. (2015). Limited faith in the good faith exception: The Third Circuit requires a warrant for GPS searches and narrows the scope of the Davis exception to the exclusionary rule in United States v. Katzin. BCL Rev., 56, 33.

Herauf, H., & Kuntz, S. (2015). Reasonableness: A case for upholding the warrantless search in Riley v. California. Adelphia LJ, 20, 79.

Huijser, M. P., Fairbank, E. R., Camel-Means, W., Graham, J., Watson, V., Basting, P., & Becker, D. (2016). The effectiveness of short sections of wildlife fencing and crossing structures along highways in reducing wildlife-vehicle collisions and providing safe crossing opportunities for large mammals. Biological Conservation, 197, 61-68.

Kamisar, Y. (2017). The Miranda case fifty years later. BUL Rev., 97, 1293.

Kerr, O. S. (2016). The effect of legislation on Fourth Amendment protection. Mich. L. Rev., 115, 1117.

Khammanivong, A., Anandharaj, A., Qian, X., Song, J. M., Upadhyaya, P., Balbo, S., & Kassie, F. (2016). Transcriptome profiling in oral cavity and esophagus tissues from (S)-N'-nitrosonornicotine-treated rats reveals candidate genes involved in human oral cavity and esophageal carcinogenesis. Molecular carcinogenesis, 55(12), 2168-2182.

Lewis, T. T. (Ed.). (2016). The US Supreme Court. Grey House Publishing.

Maclin, T. (2015). A comprehensive analysis of the history of interrogation law, with some shots directed at Miranda v. Arizona.

Meares, T. L. (2015). Programming errors: Understanding the constitutionality of stop and frisk as a program, not an incident. U. Chi. L. Rev., 82, 159.

Minnesota v. Dickerson. (n.d.). Oyez. Retrieved September 12, 2018 from https://www.oyez.org/cases/1992/91-2019.

Nowak, B., & Glenn, W. J. (2017). Searches of students' cell phones: Case analysis and best practices. Education Leadership Review of Doctoral Research, 5, 16-29.

Payton v. New York. (n.d.). Oyez. Retrieved September 12, 2018 from https://www.oyez.org/cases/1978/78-5420.

Saunders, B. A., Kelly, E., Cohen, N. P., & Guarino, C. (2016). Right-wing authoritarianism and social dominance orientation indirectly predict support for New York City's stop and frisk policy through prejudice. Current Psychology, 35(1), 92-98.

Thomas III, G. C. (2014). Mapp v. Ohio: Doomed from the beginning. Ohio St. J. Crim. L., 12, 289.

United States v. Watson. (n.d.). Oyez. Retrieved September 12, 2018 from https://www.oyez.org/cases/1975/74-538.

Walsh, P., & Sullivan, P. (2018). The Posse Comitatus Act and the Fourth Amendment's exclusionary rule. Nat'l Sec. L. Brief, 8, 3.

Walton, T. (2016). Using a mixed methods approach to investigate university student success after support service interaction: A case study and analysis. JANZSSA-Journal of the Australian and New Zealand Student Services Association, 24(2), 1094.

Whren v. United States. (n.d.). Oyez. Retrieved September 12, 2018 from https://www.oyez.org/cases/1995/95-5841.

CHAPTER THREE
COMPSTAT IN FIGHTING CRIME

Introduction

CompStat is a tool used by police officers for assistance in fighting crime. This chapter outlines CompStat, the history, purpose, principles, explanation, and effectiveness (Molinari, 2016). The combination of philosophy, management, and organizational management tools is also CompStat and used by police departments. The accountability process is implemented abroad and the United States (Stamm, 2015). CompStat is a dynamic crime reduction approach that offers personnel management, quality of life improvement, and resource management. Computer statistics are used in the police department to identify the rate of crime in the country; however, targeted enforcement is evident in the process (Molinari, 2016). In law enforcement, the term stands for 'Computer Statistics' to stop and control crime. Starting around 1994, companies began using computer-generated statistics to track success (before the development of CompStat) (Bond & Braga, 2015). The police departments started tracking crime with the assistance of CompStat; because it is an efficient tool to fight against crime.

The New York Police Department was determined to decrease the rate of crime in the early 90s but had not method to track and decreases and had no plan to reduce crime (Silverman, 2018). The information obtained from sources was old and not accurate, which is the core reason behind the development of CompStat. The critical goal of CompStat is to get accurate intelligence and information about crime. The intelligence includes the occurrence of crime, tactics, and focus of police in the area. All the information obtained by the police when crime occurs is stored in a computer program; however, the program presents the mapping of crime (Ratcliffe, 2015). Those officers having the best understanding of the situation and crime consideration are deployed to the area. For instance, using the program, when there is a drug issue, the drug unit deploys to that area and those officers who find difficulty in addressing the drug issue receive training to reduce crime (Drawve & Walker, 2018).

How Does It Work?

The process of using CompStat could be described as a police operations two-pronged examination. Through CompStat, the first prong contains effects of crime in the community outwardly, however, the other examines internal factors of the organization as well as the practices to manage risk management issues and police personnel in terms of use of force, sick time, pursuits, accompanying municipal, complaints, and liability (Skogan et al., 2015). The processing of the internal police department and examination of crime allows the reengineering of processes interlinked with the actions and public safety procedures. All these measures are essential for analyzing the performance of police (Silverman, 2018). In addition, the process contains further stages for evaluation to find results. This includes collecting, analyzing, mapping, and reviewing information about crime and the performance of the police. Using these measures aid with creating effective strategies to identify issues and apply real-time strategies (Stovall, 2015). Meanwhile, employees and police managers are accountable for the data measured and performance, repetition in the process, and consistent review. The culture of the organization keeps personnel focused over the mandate of management and organizational mission to adapt continuously to decrease crime (Roeder et al., 2015).

CompStat History

Crime was a huge concern in the early 1990s for residents of New York, and NYPD bosses wanted to improve the conditions of the city. Decreasing crime was an essential component for ensuring quality life and reducing fear. However, the former Commissioner Bratton faced several barriers trying to improve conditions (Roeder et al., 2015). In this regard, the NYPD made a purposeful attempt to collect crime statistics from the FBI. The NYPD used the collected information to analyze and maintain a systematic focus to avoid crime reporting in the city (Csurka et al., 2016). The field operations had issues because everyone was busy answering 911 calls of 911 and not an officer had time to review the conditions of the city. The effectiveness of police officers was judged based on response time, clearance rates, and arrest statistics (Skogan et al., 2015). Several jurisdictions considered the police not accountable for preventing crime in the city; therefore, having the need to implement a measurement system for data-driven performance, eventually known as CompStat (Drawve & Walker, 2018). The early system was formed to track the response of police and crime statistics described by Bill Bratton. A significant shift in the department was represented with the implementation of CompStat as well as a focus on crime prevention with a reduction in police corruption (Stovall, 2015).

Purpose of CompStat

CompStat is a famous name given to the computer files used by the police departments across the world. Study results indicate that CompStat files are tools of management for the police department for handling the affairs of law and order (Yüksel, 2014). One of the distinctive features of the CompStat is the effective mechanism of accountability in the police departments. Initially, CompStat was only used by the police departments in the US, but extended abroad (Vito, 2017).

A more significant look at the purpose of CompStat revealed that the approach of dealing with crime situations has changed. There has been a significant decrement in the rate of crime after the introduction of CompStat. The standard of living increased because of the improvement of law and order in the community (Telep, 2017). The implementation of CompStat has strengthened the linkage between police and the community. People, in general, have been very satisfied due to the tremendous improvement the situation of law and order in their environment (Slothower et al., 2015). CompStat has the capability to provide accurate and precise information to obtain adequate resources, complete tactical planning, and efficiently follow-up on crime. The productivity of law and order as a system has undergone massive changes in outlook and infrastructure to achieve the optimum level of stability due to CompStat. Hence, it is serving an essential purpose of maintaining law and order (Telep, 2016).

Four Principles of CompStat

The CompStat system emphasizes information sharing, accountability, improving effectiveness, and responsibility. CompStat comprises of four core components a) relentless follow up, b) effective tactics, c) accurate timely intelligence and information, and d) rapid resources development (Sherman, 2018). CompStat is a classic method problem-solving solution that focuses on the level of accountability of an organization. The statically quantifiable indicators, the CompStat evaluate the clusters, crime patterns, suspects, crime patterns, and hot spots (Myers et al., 2014). The basic strategies are formulated to control the crime ratio. The development strategies and creativity are encouraged by the CompStat process as well as deploying personnel and allocating resources (Molinari, 2016). Using CompStat causes employees and managers accountability in case of problem confrontment of the crime-pro activity. The model of the CompStat business management system comprises of four setups that confine the crime resolution strategies to give security system cost-effective operations (Aleo, 2017). The four principles are the analysis and the collection of timely and accurate intelligence, rapid development, effective ticktack's development, and the operations assessments (Lump & Koper, 2014). The identification process and profiling require timely and accurate intelligence for emerging crime issues and the assessment of the effort's resolution. The crime problem resolution process requires tactic development through implementation and action plans. The tactics plan establishment in order to encounter and identify crime and the command personnel is deploying the complete plan before action execution (Kelling & Coles, 2017).

Effectiveness of CompStat

The process of CompStat was implemented eleven years before in New York City, and it is known as an active process to fight against crime. After the story of New York, other cities initiated similar programs. The effectiveness of CompStat is indicted through statistical information to reduce crime; however, the efficacy of the system and programs is still a question (Csurka et al., 2016). Contemporary policing would be revolutionized with the CompStat program that was initially created as a software package for a small business named SmartWare. The primary focus of the program was the establishment of a statistical baseline with the major incidents counted to identify criminal activities by mapping the clusters (de Maillard, 2018). The NYPD officers of the Rudolph Giuliani administration named the program and process. William Bratton implemented the program in 1994 as Giuliani's 1st police commissioner. The policing considered as an innovative managerial paradigm winner of Innovations in American Government award 1996 (Eterno et al., 2017). Each precinct Bratton wanted to collect information on crime data went into a computer database every week and a disk with the information submitted to the police commissioner's office. The criminal activity was the responsibility of every commander in his precinct to state a plan of required improvement. Jack Maple assigned a deputy commissioner and a startup team to review the process. A considerable improvement was seen after the implementation of the program (Pasha & Kroll, 2016).

Crime Mapping and Effectiveness

The CompStat stands for the computer comparison statics and is a multifaceted setup developed to monitor police operations. The function of CompStat is to control crime by monitoring functions such as, meetings usually/weekly used to identify the performance indicators of the agency to show efficacy by effectively reviewing information (Sherman, 2018). The analyst utilizes the crime mapping system in law enforcement agencies to map, analyze, and visualize the patterns of crime incidents. The crime mapping is the crucial factor in the crime analysis and CompStat strategy (Myers et al., 2014). The crime mapping is dependent on the geographic information system (GIS) that enables the crime analyst to distinguish the crime while including the hot spots, patterns, and trends. The research and policies perspectives denote that the crime mapping is used to implement the patterns by understanding the recidivism and incarceration, which help programs, target resources, crime reduction programs, and evaluation of the crime prevention strategies (Sherman, 2018). The latest internet technologies, specifically GIS provides opportunities to implement the crime mapping system to support crime prevention. The web crime mapping widely focuses on community support policing instead of analytical functions, analysis pattern, and prediction (Slothower et al., 2015).

Evidence-Based Policing

According to the basic concept of the evidence-based policing, CompStat gives an overall layout for the staff at police stations to meet the needs, requirements, and challenges of the day to day affairs of the law enforcing agency (Cordner, 2018). The evidence-based policing is also regarded as a tactical tool for making critical decisions on the matters of law and order in society. Police staff have been introduced to scientific testing of the crime scenes, evidence, and criminal approaches to track down the criminals (Bond & Braga, 2015). There is not a second opinion to suggest policing has been managed effectively with the presence of evidence-based policing by acting within the limits of available resources. Different countries have used evidence-based policing for different purposes (Cordner, 2018). For instance, evidence-based policing can be used to uplift the morale of the police staff by working on the education and enforcement level of the police. The rates of sentences can also be examined by evidence-based policing to include the determination of the degree and frequency of the punishments to the criminals by the police department (Kelling & Coles, 2017).

Intelligence-Led Policing

Explanation

Intelligence-led policing was developed from crime-fighting philosophies and contains community policing, CompStat, problem-oriented policing, and accountability mechanism. The degree of the distinct mechanism was used to define the role, analysis, and establishment of CompStat decision making (Vito et al., 2017). The street-level police and bottom-up philosophy is a vital part of problem-oriented policing to identify and resolve problems at the forefront. The hierarchical steps of intelligence-led policing emphasize the top-down law enforcement approach. At the executive level, the flow of criminal intelligence was restricted to the decision makers to set up prevention and priorities for the operational tasking at the lower level (Santos, 2014). The differences in the led policing are developed with intelligence from community policing. This is considered as incompatible for community contact, community policing, philosophy, and empowerment (Bond & Braga, 2015). While the needs and desires of the local community are emphasized through determined priorities and strategies based on the criminal environment. Such factors are analyzed through developed objectives prioritized on crime reduction features in the community (Stamm, 2015).

Effectiveness

The organization of the policies and philosophies aid with integrating effectiveness in the community and enhancing effectiveness to improve law enforcement decision making. The integration and configuration were the baseline for short-term success attained by police agencies (Molinari, 2016). Cultural factors were considered in the process of implementing and adopting the program. Rate of offenders reduced drastically, and legal implications resolved with the role of the team appreciated in regards with enforcing CompStat and obtaining favorable results (Eterno et al., 2017).

Chapter Summary

The crime was a huge concern in the early 1990s for residents of New York because of bad conditions. New York's police chief wanted to improve the conditions of the city to ensure quality life and reduce fear. The combination of philosophy, management, and organizational management tools is known as CompStat, which is used by the police departments. CompStat is a dynamic crime reduction approach that offers personnel management, quality of life improvement and resource management. Comparative statistics are used in the police department to identify the rate of crime in the country; however, targeted enforcement is evident in the process. The early system was formed to track the response of police and crime statistics described by Bill Bratton. The New York Police Department was determined to decrease the rate of crime in the early 90s, but they had nothing to track things accurately and had no plan to reduce crime. A more significant look at the purpose of the CompStat revealed that the approach of dealing with crime situations has changed because of it. There has been a significant decrement in the rate of crime after the introduction of CompStat. The CompStat comprises of four core components that includes relentless follow up, effective tactics, accurate and timely intelligence and information, and rapid resources development to emphasize information sharing, accountability, and improving effectiveness and responsibility. The analyst utilizes the crime mapping system in law enforcement agencies to map, analyze, and visualize the patterns of crime incidents. The role of an individual team is appreciated as a means to enforce CompStat and obtain favorable results.

References

Aleo, C. (Ed.). (2017). Critical Perspectives on Effective Policing and Police Brutality. Enslow Publishing, LLC.

Bond, B. J., & Braga, A. A. (2015). Rethinking the Comp stat process to enhance problem-solving responses: Insights from a randomized field experiment. *Police Practice and Research*, *16*(1), 22-35.

Cordner, G. (2018). A practical approach to evidence based policing. *Evidence Based Policing: An Introduction*, 231.

Csurka, G., Larlus, D., Gordo, A., & Almazan, J. (2016). What is the right way to represent document images?. arXiv preprint arXiv:1603.01076.

de Maillard, J. (2018). Police performance regimes and police activity: CompStat in Paris and London compared. European Journal of Criminology, 1477370817749497.

Drawve, G. R., & Walker, J. T. (2018). What is crime analysis?. In Foundations of Crime Analysis (pp. 18-34). Routledge.

Eterno, J. A., Barrow, C. S., & Silverman, E. B. (2017). Forcible stops: Police and citizens speak out. Public Administration Review, 77(2), 181-192.

Kelling, G. L., & Coles, C. M. (2017). COMMUNITY POLICING IN THE 21ST CENTURY: A FRAMEWORK FOR MEASURING PERFORMANCE. *URBAN POLICY FRONTIERS*, 29.

Lump, C., & Koper, C. S. (2014). Evidence-based policing. In *Encyclopedia of criminology and criminal justice* (pp. 1426-1437). Springer, New York, NY.

Molinari, M. C. (2016). *Implementing Comp Stat principles into critical infrastructure protection and improvement*. Naval Postgraduate School Monterey United States.

Myers, L., Parrish, A., & Williams, A. (2014). Big Data and the Fourth Amendment: Reducing Overreliance on the Objectivity of Predictive Policing. *Fed. Cts. L. Rev., 8*, 231.

Pasha, O., & Kroll, A. (2016). The Effectiveness of CompStat Systems: An Interrupted Time Series Analysis of Crime in US Cities. In Academy of Management Proceedings (Vol. 2016, No. 1, p. 14713). Briarcliff Manor, NY 10510: Academy of Management.

Ratcliffe, J. (2015). What is the future... of predictive policing? Practice, 6(2), 151-166.

Roeder, O., Eisen, L. B., Bowling, J., Stiglitz, J., & Chettiar, I. (2015). What Caused the Crime Decline?.

Santos, R. B. (2014). The effectiveness of crime analysis for crime reduction: Cure or diagnosis?. Journal of Contemporary Criminal Justice, 30(2), 147-168.

Sherman, L. W. (2018). Evidence-based policing: Social organization of information for social control. In *Crime and social organization* (pp. 235-266). Routledge.

Silverman, B. W. (2018). Density estimation for statistics and data analysis. Routledge.

Skogan, W. G., Van Craen, M., & Hennessy, C. (2015). Training police for procedural justice. Journal of experimental criminology, 11(3), 319-334.

Slothower, M., Sherman, L. W., & Neyroud, P. (2015). Tracking quality of police actions in a victim contact program: A case study of training, tracking, and feedback (TTF) in evidence-based policing. *International Criminal Justice Review*, *25*(1), 98-116.

Stamm, E. (2015). Methods of Policing: Deviation from the Standard Model of Policing and Measured Effectiveness.

Stovall, D. (2015). Community policing: re-evaluating what has become a program instead of a paradigm shift.

Telep, C. W. (2016). Expanding the scope of evidence-based policing. *Criminology & Public Policy*, *15*(1), 243-252.

Telep, C. W. (2017). Police officer receptivity to research and evidence-based policing: examining variability within and across agencies. *Crime & delinquency*, *63*(8), 976-999.

Vito, G. F., Reed, J. C., & Walsh, W. F. (2017). Police executives' and managers' perspectives on Comp stat. *Police Practice and Research*, *18*(1), 15-25.

YÜKSEL, Y. (2014). IMPLEMENTATION OF COMPSTAT IN POLICE ORGANIZATIONS: THE CASE OF NEWARK POLICE DEPARTMENT. *Journal of International Social Research*, *7*(35).

CHAPTER FOUR
KANSAS CITY PREVENTIVE PATROL AND KANSAS CITY GUN EXPERIMENT

Introduction

The empirical validity of police patrol was tested through the Kansas City Preventive Patrol Experiment. Police patrol is considered as one of the key strategies used in the services and applications of modern policing. The strategy contains routine, motorized, visible, and random patrol as steps. Patrol activities are assigned to police personnel around 60 to 65 percent in the modern democratic societies. In some studies, the objective of the strategy is to deter crime, reduce crime fear, and arrest offenders. The strategy ingrained in the early 70s due to less credible evidence and no precise measurement presented to demonstrate the efficiency of the strategy. The foundation of police includes researchers, task force, and evidence gaps. The development and implementation of experimental investigation design tests the effectiveness of routine preventive patrols. The report includes the Kanas City Preventive Patrol experiment to present the effectiveness and limitations of the experiment through explaining, analyzing, and concluding the points. However, it is essential to elaborate on the effectiveness integrated into the projects after the implementation of the project.

Meanwhile, the contribution of the experiment for the police department will be investigated in further sections.

Explanation

In July 1972, implementation of the experiment started, and several problems were recognized by the Kansas City Police Department and the police foundation. These issues fundamentally exposed the integrity of the experiment. Initially, the problem was low human resources for the experiment that was caused by the South Patrol Division (Carriaga & Worrall, 2015). However, to get rid of this limitation several police officers were involved in the process. Furthermore, violation of the guidelines was the other issue that affected the credibility of the experiment. Officers used for the purpose were not following the guidelines carefully were not accepting any assigned duty but giving a response to service call (Ratcliffe et al., 2015). In addition, training was provided, and directorial measures considered ensuring adherence to the guidelines. These issues were effectively monitored to limit the consequences of the experiment and obtain useful results (Novak et al., 2015).

Another problem from the experiment was boredom amongst the assigned officers because of "reactive" beats. The issues were countered by modifying the guidelines and increasing activities amongst the officers to change "reactive" assigned to "proactive" beats (Carriaga & Worrall, 2015). Adherence of the guidelines was stressed after revising the components, which managed the spirit of the project instead of unalterable rules. For some time the experiment stopped and in October 1972 resumed, until September 1973 it was successfully continued. Stress was given to the components of findings shaped to investigate the effects of the experiment on the measured outcome (Novak et al., 2016). The following questions were asked in the experiment:

- Would the citizens notice a change in the patrol police?
- Is there any change recorded or visible for the levels of police patrol or results obtained from victim surveys?
- Is there any change in the attendant behavior and citizen's crime fear as a result of different patrol levels?
- Is there a change in the degree of satisfaction with a change in the police?

To get answers for the question information was collected from reported crime rates, victimization surveys, arrest data, attitudinal surveys, a survey of local businesses, and trained observers for monitoring the interaction of police-citizen (Piza & O'Hara, 2014).

Analysis

Because of this experiment, it was found that there is no noticeable change in the three experimental conditions used to report victimization, recorded crime, citizens' fear of crime, police response time, citizen satisfaction for police service, traffic accidents, arrests, and some other significant indicators (Ratcliffe & Sorg, 2017). In particular, there was no change in the recorded experimental conditions in terms of non-residence burglaries, larcenies, auto thefts, vandalism, or robberies, to deter patrol prevention. In terms of crime reporting rates to the police, there were no consistent patterns and few differences occurred within the experimental conditions (Weisburd & Telep, 2014). In terms of the crimes reported and recorded, there was one set of differences within the conditions of an experiment judged based on random occurrence. Meanwhile, there were few significant differences without having any consistent patterns followed by the experimental conditions to state attitudes regarding police services (Novak et al., 2015). Because of citizens' fear of crime, the experimental conditions did not affect the overall city environment. However, as the results of the experiment indicated no consistent pattern, while, few differences were seen in terms of the types and number of anticrime protective measures employed in the city (Piza & O'Hara, 2014). In general, the experimental conditions did not affect the services of police and crime. The dealing of the problem was successful in attempting and targeting numerous issues and these programs stopped crime (Ratcliffe & Sorg, 2017). The satisfaction of citizens was not altered by the use of experimental conditions through the police or from encounters with officers. There was no significant effect identified in the response time of citizens because of the experimental conditions used in the city. Meanwhile, no change was found in the injuries or traffic accidents across the experimental conditions. Therefore, experimental conditions were having a positive impact on the city as crime and fear reduced and citizen satisfaction maintained by the police officers (Carriaga & Worrall, 2015).

Effectiveness

A visible presence was created by the police that deterred offenders while, the development of the telephone and radio changed tactics of police patrol to make them proactive instead of reactive. Results indicated the police were wondering to form a visible presence, as it was essential to deter the offenders (Weisburd & Telep, 2014). Awareness about the patrol zones was given to community policing to develop strategies to meet the expectations of the experiment. Meanwhile, information was provided regarding the acts of terrorists and terrorism (Weisburd, 2018). In this way, event analysis was utilized by the police for target-oriented optimization. A similar experiment was followed in connection to the experiment known as the Kansas City experiment and planned to target the hot spots of crime. However, a large amount of data regarding the crime was utilized in the process of analyzing and identifying the hot spots of crime (Braga & Weisburd, 2015). At that time, the crime occurred at particular places and parts of the city and these hot spots were targeted through the directed patrol. Police became highly focused on the hot spots and problems going on in those areas. There were different features and components used for drunk driving, guns, and gang violence (Telep et al., 2016). The police dealt with the issues by targeting specific issues using programs that eventually ended the crime in the country. The response of traditional police against domestic violence was smooth and family matters or personal matters avoided (Kelling, 2015). The police department used the policies found within the Minneapolis study and made arrest mandatory within the policies. In these practices, dual arrests of both parties occurred by the police officers in cases of domestic violence (Weisburd & Telep, 2014).

Limitations

The police pursuing issue made it hard for the department to check and reevaluate policies, there were limitations in some jurisdictions with decreasing violent felonies (Braga et al., 2014). Foot pursuits were used for training purposes as a method of improving apprehenshion methods that, decreased injury for the officers and their suspects. The operations and functions of detectives changed, causing the detectives to wear hats because this job involves intelligence gathering operations, undercover operations, and all types of crime investigation (Weisburd et al., 2015). All the initial reports were monitored and followed by the investigator as they attempted to put recent developments and puzzles pieces together to find physical evidence (Weisburd, 2018). This approached solved the puzzle and the suspects were track down with DNA and an automated fingerprint identification system used by the investigators. However, after review, the police used entrapment and enticement (Braga & Weisburd, 2015), and failed to follow the guidelines carefully because were accepting assigned duty but responding to a service call. Furthermore, police should not commit crime but, stop crime. These are the limitations identified in the Kansas City Preventive Patrol Experiment (Kelling, 2015).

Conclusion

The analysis conducted determined that the objective of the patrol activity was to deter crime, reduce crime fear, and arrest offenders. Meanwhile, there were some steps followed that included routine, motorized, visible, and random patrol. The development of the strategy was ingrained in the early 70s to ensure the efficiency of the strategy through precise measurement and credible evidence interlinked with the experimental conditions. The primary factors considered in the process revolved around the task force and evidence gap factors. The development and implementation of experimental investigation design test the effectiveness of routine preventive patrol. The design of the experiment was based on the problems and conditions of New York City and was essential for the police department to rectify those issues for smooth flow of security in the city. There was a time in which restrictions were made to continue the experiment because the departments continued to improve.

Meanwhile, the experiment had both positive and negative effects on experimental conditions. The positive results are known as effectiveness and negative results, limitations. Information was collected from a variety of sources for analysis, while, the police officers became motivated and proactive. Change in the policies and practices occurred to ensure the allocation of the experiment within the city. However, at times, guidelines were not followed by the police, affected the credibility of the results, causing another limitation. As a concluding note, the results of the experiment included crime deduction and changes to police discipline when failing to follow department guidelines.

Kansas City Gun Experiment

The famous gun experiment was the Kansas City Gun Experiment of 1991 and the New York Police Department believed this experiment reduced the use of guns in the city. Furthermore, the objective was to limit violence by homicide and shootings. Various critical factors became a part of the experiment, creating difficulty in obtaining useful results for strategies and solutions. To perform targeted activities and experiments, the police used certain places and hot spots. Attention was given to places in the city associated with the beat of patrol and the district of the patrol. Leaders made assumptions to resolve problems based on the experiment. This increased the opportunity to target any hot spot. In this report, the experiment discussed is for understanding the effectiveness and limitations by analyzing the Kansas City Gun Experiment.

Explanation

Police patrol project was infamous with the Kansas City Gun Experiment and the aim was to reduce the violence associated with guns such as, homicides and drive-by shootings (Ridgeway, 2018). Gun violence was the critical issue in the city that needed attention and strategies to be resolved, so the experiment became the solution. Furthermore, the marked zone in the experiment of the gun was the beat of patrol around 144 in the dominant Kansas City, MO (Rostron, 2016). The spot had the second peak drive of the shooting of the district patrol in 1991. Moreover, the target beat was around 80 by 10 in the block area with a rate of homicide of 177 per 100,000 individuals, which was 20 times more than the national average. All this description was followed to ensure effective results for the experiment (Koper & Lum, 2017).

The experiment in Kansas City was based on the assumption that gun crime and gun seizures are not directly related, yet, the increasing of one directly decreases the other (Weisburd, 2016). Furthermore, it can be explained that the increase of gun seizures decreases the crime of gun. Two possible mechanisms can easily explain this connection between incapacitating and deterrence (Koper & Lum, 2017). The deterrence theory of assumption describes that if it remained to develop known that rule implementation is likely to seize the guns and unlawful and prohibited gun haulers, which would be less probable to carry the guns in this specific area (Rostron, 2016). Whereas, deterrence theory proposes that increasing the visibility of patrol in an area will dissuade the crime while clarifying the intentions and association of the elements (Ridgeway, 2018).

Analysis

The analysis section of the Kansas City Gun Experiment consists of the following steps and each of the steps was followed in the experimental conditions to ensure effective and supportive results for the patrol department.

Gun Seizures

Observing six months, the number of guns seized was 1,000 per residents in the targeted and the beat of comparison (Weisburd, 2016).

Trends in Gun Crimes

In 29 weeks, there were approximately 169 crimes committed with guns in a specified area after starting hot spots on the patrols and only 86 of the crimes found in 29 weeks in the patrol of phase 1. This variation was of great importance statistically as it includes two of the different methods of analysis (Wu & Wells, 2016).

Displacement

While the gun crimes dropped in the beat of 144, none of the other seven adjacent beats pragmatic a single critical increment in the crime of gun. Furthermore, some of the evidence suggested the program provided benefits to the police department (Lum & Nagin, 2017).

Drive-by Shootings

Examination displayed that the drive by shootings declined during six months when police were found active in different places mainly the hot spots as compared with the patrols not in the designated periods (Mason, 2015).

Homicides

Homicides increased during the period in which the patrol services were not active. No significant alteration found in homicides from the crossways of those time durations in comparison to beat and contagious beat (Wu & Wells, 2016).

Other Crimes

Not any substantial variation found in the board or the area of contrast on entire calls for the services of police in which the violence calls were also mentioned.

Primarily efforts were made to ensure that the surroundings had no problems from the experiment as well as to manage the order (Ridgeway, 2018).

Effectiveness

The patrolling projects for the police have been under constant improvisation to improve conditions. The Kansas Gun Experiment aimed to reduce the violence created by the guns because of significant evidence of drive-by shootings and homicides in the state (Koper & Lum, 2017). Therefore, the program was implemented to ensure a peaceful environment for the people in the state of Kansas. After carefully examining the situation developed after the implementation of the Kansas Gun Experiment, it became inevitable to explore the effectiveness and limitations of the project (Weisburd, 2016)

The program was quite useful because a significant number of weapons were seized from different locations of the state. Police officials detained huge number guns at an individual level in a short period. The guns presences in the state reduced by 65% in the state of Kansas (Mason, 2015). There was a sharp decline in the rate of crime as well with the presence of criminals decreased too. The public took was convinced that the active preventive measures used by the police limited the number guns in the state (Lum & Nagin, 2017). The entire community had taken sufficient comfort because of the significant changes brought by the Kansas Guns Experiment. In the past, several incidents were reported related to drive by shootings and had resulted in several casualties (Hoover et al., 2016). With the enforcement of the program, these incidents decreased, resulting in a peaceful situation. Furthermore, the number of homicides decreased because of the active patrolling from the police in the area (Rydberg et al., 2018).

Limitations

Unfortunately, despite the significant developments obtained from the Kansas Guns Experiment in New York, there was a full outrage cry in the media that the experiment had failed to cripple down the large criminals of the state (Lum & Nagin, 2017). It was the primary consideration from the results obtained for the experiment at that time. Several people found it harsh to experiment without any gain. As the people who were arrested or targeted during the experiment were still roaming freely in the state (Hoover et al., 2016). In addition to that, the guns confiscated were mainly in the urban areas. The results also indicated the actual number and dangerous forms of weapons were still in the safe zones and used by criminals (Rydberg et al., 2018). Alternative techniques were also discovered to bluff the police over the possession of the guns in the state and they had easily bypassed the guns experiment conducted by the police in the state of New York.

Moreover, there was no decrease in kidnapping using the Kansas Guns Experiment (Meares, 2015). These results revealed that crime was still present in the state and the objective of the experiment was not attained in any form. Another area left unchecked was smuggling, which occurred on the superhighways and main drive-by (Braga, 2014). Perhaps, many flaws were evident in the role and strategies used in the Kansas City Gun Experiment. The targeted people were still out of the control of the police; therefore, because of the whole elucidation the limitations should be converted into the effectiveness of the Kansas program (Hoover et al., 2016).

Conclusion

In conclusion, the Kansas City Gun Experiment followed specific assumptions that states there is no direct connection between gun crime and seizures. These factors have an inverse connection because an increase of one decreases the other. Incapacitation and deterrence are the two factors that explain the connection between the assumptions. Furthermore, it is identified that there were some steps or stages followed in the experiment that includes gun seizures, trends in gun crimes, displacement, drive-by shootings, homicides, and other crimes. The results indicated from the effectiveness of the experiment that the program has great importance in history due to a significant number of weapons seized at hot spots of the state. A large number of guns were detained during the process of the experiment at an individual level. The results indicate 65% of gun presence reduced in the state of Kansas, as well as street-level crimes and homicides decreased. However, there were some flaws in the implementation of the experiment including the control of the police in the state and the possession of the gun. Overall, the efficiency of the results was high in contrast with the applications, functions, and features of the experiment, which supported a reduction in crime.

Chapter Summary

The analysis conducted on the Kansas City Preventive Patrol experiment stemmed from the objective to deter crime, reduce crime fear and arrest offenders. The experiment steps included routine, motorized, visible, and random patrol. The development of the strategies ingrained in the early 70s to ensure efficiency through precise measurement and credible evidence interlinked with the experimental conditions. The patrolling projects for the police have been under constant improvisation to make things better. The Kansas Gun Experiment was aimed to reduce gun violence in the US. The program implementation to ensure a peaceful environment for the people in the state of Kansas. Unfortunately, despite the significant developments obtained using the Kansas Guns Experiment in the state of New York, confiscated guns in urban areas.

Moreover, the activities such as kidnapping for ransom did not decrease because of the Kansas Guns Experiment. However, the program was quite useful because a significant number of weapons seized from different locations of the state. The police officials detained huge numbers of guns at an individual level in a short period. The guns presences in the state reduced by 65% in the state of Kansas with a sharp decline in the rate of crime and the presence of criminals decreased too. Overall, the public was convinced that the police limited the guns in the state.

References

Braga, A. A., & Weisburd, D. L. (2015). Police innovation and crime prevention: Lessons learned from police research over the past 20 years.

Braga, A. A., Papachristos, A. V., & Hureau, D. M. (2014). The effects of hot spots policing on crime: An updated systematic review and meta-analysis. *Justice quarterly*, *31*(4), 633-663.

Carriaga, M. L., & Worrall, J. L. (2015). Police levels and crime: a systematic review and meta-analysis. *The Police Journal*, *88*(4), 315-333.

Hoover, L., Wells, W., Zhang, Y., Ren, L., & Zhao, J. (2016). Houston enhanced action patrol: examining the effects of differential deployment lengths with a switched replication design. *Justice Quarterly*, *33*(3), 538-563.

Kelling, G. (2015). An author's brief history of an idea. *Journal of Research in Crime and Delinquency*, *52*(4), 626-629.

Koper, C. S., & Lum, C. (2017). Place-Based Policing. *Policing 2026 Evidence Review*, 37.

Lum, C., & Nagin, D. S. (2017). Reinventing american policing. *Crime and justice*, *46*(1), 339-393.

Mason, K. J. (2015). *An analysis of the effects of proactive policing on drug offenses in a university campus environment*. Lamar University-Beaumont.

Meares, T. L. (2015). Programming errors: Understanding the constitutionality of stop-and-frisk as a program, not an incident. *U. Chi. L. Rev., 82*, 159.

Novak, K. J., Fox, A. M., Carr, C. M., & Spade, D. A. (2016). The efficacy of foot patrol in violent places. *Journal of Experimental Criminology, 12*(3), 465-475.

Novak, K. J., Fox, A. M., Carr, C. M., McHale, J., & White, M. D. (2015). *Kansas City, Missouri Smart Policing Initiative: From Foot Patrol to Focused Deterrence.* CNA.

Piza, E. L., & O'Hara, B. A. (2014). Saturation foot-patrol in a high-violence area: A quasi-experimental evaluation. *Justice Quarterly, 31*(4), 693-718.

Ratcliffe, J. H., & Sorg, E. T. (2017). A History of Foot Patrol. In *Foot Patrol* (pp. 7-20). Springer, Cham.

Ratcliffe, J. H., Groff, E. R., Sorg, E. T., & Haberman, C. P. (2015). Citizens' reactions to hot spots policing: impacts on perceptions of crime, disorder, safety and police. *Journal of experimental criminology, 11*(3), 393-417.

Ridgeway, G. (2018). Experiments in Criminology: Improving Our Understanding of Crime and the Criminal Justice System. *Annual Review of Statistics and Its Application,* (0).

Rostron, A. (2016). A new state ice age for gun policy. *Harv. L. & Pol'y Rev., 10*, 327.

Rydberg, J., McGarrell, E. F., Norris, A., & Circo, G. (2018). A quasi-experimental synthetic control evaluation of a place-based police-directed patrol intervention on violent crime. *Journal of Experimental Criminology, 14*(1), 83-109.

Telep, C. W., Weisburd, D., Wire, S., & Farrington, D. (2016). Protocol: Increased Police Patrol Presence Effects on Crime and Disorder.

Weisburd, D. (2016). Does hot spots policing inevitably lead to unfair and abusive police practices, or can we maximize both fairness and effectiveness in the new proactive policing. *U. Chi. Legal F.*, 661.

Weisburd, D. (2018). Hot spots of crime and place-based prevention. *Criminology & Public Policy, 17*(1), 5-25.

Weisburd, D., & Telep, C. W. (2014). Hot spots policing: What we know and what we need to know. *Journal of Contemporary Criminal Justice, 30*(2), 200-220.

Weisburd, D., Groff, E. R., Jones, G., Cave, B., Amendola, K. L., Yang, S. M., & Emison, R. F. (2015). The Dallas patrol management experiment: can AVL technologies be used to harness unallocated patrol time for crime prevention?. *Journal of Experimental Criminology, 11*(3), 367-391.

Wu, L., & Wells, W. (2016). A micro-level analysis of firearm arrests' effects on gun violence in Houston, Texas. *GeoJournal, 81*(6), 891-905.

CHAPTER FIVE

DEATH PENALTY IN UNITED STATES

Introduction

The death penalty, also known as capital execution, occurs when the state or government executes someone for committing a crime. Generally, research suggested the death penalty does not offer a chance of improvement and consideration for the criminal while alternatives to the death penalty are not as strict. The alternatives offer an opportunity for criminals to improve behavior; however, studies conducted on the subject revealed that the death penalty reduced the chances of crime and criminal activities. Researchers found that reduction in ratios is due to the criminal justice system associated with the condition. The occurrence of criminal activities is expected because of alternatives and there will be no effective means of improving the conditions of crime in the United States. However, there are legal rights incorporated under the law to maintain equality and justice for all. There are various considerations, steps focused and implemented in the states by authorities to manage equality for minorities while the alternatives to the death penalty do not seem practical. The report contains a discussion on the death penalty in the United States and the focus is on different elements associated with the topic. Several cases are included to understand the subject more effectively.

Death Penalty Methods Around the World

The death penalty, also known as capital execution, occurs when the state or government executes someone for a serious criminal charge. A crime in which a person could receive the death penalty is a capital offense or capital crime (Hood & Hoyle, 2015).

Hanging

One of the critical applied methods for the death penalty is hanging. Hanging a criminal through the death penalty is still used in several countries. Hanging causes neck fracture and instant conscious loss and is used in Singapore, India, and Japan (Steiker & Steiker, 2015).

Shooting

Shooting is a standard method of the death penalty and can be applied in many ways. Asingle shot in the neck shot occurs in China and Russia. Firing squad through the death penalty is in Russia. Excessively powerful anti-craft guns are used as the primary source of the death penalty in North Korea (James & Cossman, 2017).

Lethal Injections

Lethal injection is often considered as the least cruel method of the death penalty. Lethal dose injection is the primary death penalty method in the United States and used in five other countries such as Thailand, Taiwan, China, Vietnam, and Guatemala (Simon, 2017).

Electrocution

Electrocution is capital punishment method with the US being the only country to use the method in 2013. Electrocution is the electric chair mode of the death penalty (Reckless, 2017).

Gas Inhalation

The US and Lithuania implemented the gas inhalation method for the death penalty. Gas inhalation is legal in some states of the US (Steiker & Steiker, 2015).

Statistical Analysis of The Death Penalty In The US

Executions in the United States recorded low levels in the year 2017. The public support in terms of the death penalty in the US decreased. As per the report released by the US Death Penalty Information Centre (DPIC), eight states attempted 23 executions that are half the number of previous years. The ratio recorded is the second lowest death penalty ratio since 1991 (Reckless, 2017).

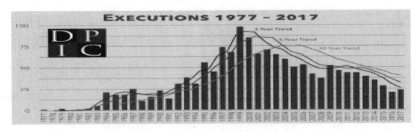

Figure 1: Death execution rate 1977-2017 (Morone, & Kersh, 2016)

In the year 2016, only six executions were attempted. In the United States, fourteen states and the federal government imposed 39 death penalty sentences in the year 2017 that was the second less annual death sentences since in the US. The United States Supreme Court declared the death penalty constitutional in 1972. It was in row seventeenth row that was fewer than 100 death penalties were imposed in the United States (Steiker & Steiker, 2015).

The modifications in Harris County, Texas became symbolic of the long-term modifications for capital punishment in the US. First time since 1974, the state completed more executions than other states that do not execute the prisoner and sentence any defendants to death as claimed by Robert Dunham, executive director of DPICs (Kastellec, 2016).

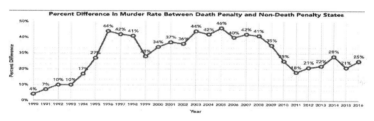

Figure 2: Death penalty ratio (James, & Cossman, 2017)

Across the United States, the political spectrum revealed that more people strive to know better procedures to keep safe than offender's executions that are selected from the random death penalty. Since 1990 in the United States, the death penalty has become obsolete. DPIC gives analysis about death penalty rates and track data and the organization has no position against or for capital punishment (Steiker & Steiker, 2015).

101

The new death penalty sentence imposed in the year 2017 indicated the increased geographical arbitrary and isolation of the death penalty in the US. Dunham stated that three countries were responsible for more than the thirty percent of the deaths imposed in US (Morone & Kersh, 2016).

The US scheduled 81 executions in the year 2017 and 70% were not accomplished. Around 75 percent of executions were in four major states, Texas completed 7 executions, Arkansas 4, Florida 3, and Alabama 3. The state court in Texas stayed seven executions by implementing new state laws permitting those prisoners to gather the false judicial reviews or the misleading evidence. The total execution tied in 2016 was for fewest conducts in the US since 1996 (Hood & Hoyle, 2015).

The systemic problems according to the racial discrimination, fraudulent or flawed forensic testimony, prosecutorial misconduct, and inadequate legal representation contributed to 2017 exonerations. The previous issues cause a change in the ratio of death and is the leading causes behind the occurrence of exonerations in the United States (Simon, 2017).

Why the Death Penalty? Does It Work?

The death penalty is the legal process established worldwide allowing a state the freedom to sentence a criminal to death. The death penalty survey held in 2009 by the leading criminologist in the US found that the overwhelming majority did not believe using the death penalty does not decrease homicides (Shirley & Gelman,

2015). Eighty-eight criminologist do not believe the death penalty works as a homicide deterrent. According to criminology studies, the abolition of the death penalty has no marked effect on murder rates (Kastellec, 2016). Therefore, 75% of the study respondent that the debates regarding death penalty majorly distracted state legislatures and Congress from concentrating the real solutions of the crime problems. The death penalty is implicated overwhelmingly in case of the working class, marginalized groups, and ethnic minorities. The death penalty system worldwide attempts to deter individuals from attempting any critical crime (Dekker, 2017).

Death Penalty Works as Crime Determinant

The surveys held on the crime death penalty determinants in the state indicated a decrease in the United States. Results revealed that 94% found in evidence was in support of useful determinant through the death penalty (Simon, 2017). In 2004 people claimed that 62 percent of the death penalty was a deterrent (Shirley & Gelman, 2015).

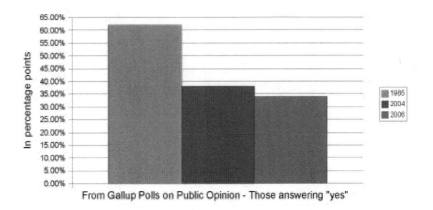

Figure 3: crime deterrent (Kastellec, 2016)

The United States for the nine consecutive years was the only country to accomplished executions in the region. The total number of executions was 23 and total death sentences are 41 in the United States (Dekker, 2017). Therefore, the death penalty remained within historically low trends of recent years. The second time since the year 2006, the US did not feature among the top five worldwide executioners, with its execution position in the worldwide ranking dropping from 7th to *th (Hood & Hoyle, 2015).

Case Analysis

a. Crampton v. Ohio Case Analysis

A black man, McCleskey was sentenced of armed robbery and the murder of a white police officer in the Fulton County Superior Court in Georgia in 1978 (Fareed et al., 2015). McCleskey confessed that he was involved in the robbery but not the murder of the police officer. During his trial, the state proved that at least one of the bullets in the gun used to shoot to the police officer was fired from McClesky's gun (Gross-Manos et al., 2018).

Moreover, the state also introduced two witnesses who had heard that McClesky murder of a police officer. The court recommended the penalty of death (Zalman, 2016). McClesky v Kemp is considered a final decision taken by the jury because it shields the system of criminal justice from racial bias claims. The scrutiny shielded a smoking gun is proof of racial discrimination in the criminal justice system, which has been proven by the study of Baldus in the McClesky case (Fareed et al. 2015). This case of a black man has been criticized several times. Justice Powell regretted his vote in this case after his retirement (Gross-Manos et al., 2018).

b. Jackson v. Georgia Case Analysis

Elmer Branch was sentenced for the crime of rape in Texas. The jury in his case was not mandated to vote for the penalty of death by law and were not given particular criteria for making decisions on the death penalty. Justice Douglas who was also involved in this case concluded that Branch's death penalty was applied disproportionately because he was poor and was socially disadvantaged (Toth, 2016). This disproportion and discrimination indicated that the fourteen amendments and Equal Protection Clause should be applied for striking down the penalty of death because the inequality among the criminals was cruel. The opinion of Justice Douglas contributed towards raising the possibility of making the proportionate decision a constitutional crime's punishment Jackson v. Virginia, 443 U.S. 307, 99 S. Ct. 2781, 61 L. Ed. 2d 560 (1979).

On the other hand, another Justice, Stewart said that death should be administered without discrimination and rationally because death is different and cruel as compared to other punishments (Toth, 2016). The Justice did not accept the absolutist position of the Branch and voted to oppose the death penalty of Branch because he thought that his death penalty was imposed mercurially. The Juries of Court involved in this rape case ignored the law for deciding on imposing the death penalty. According to Stewart, the result of this death penalty decision was cruel. The death penalty sentence for Branch was unusual and cruel and lead to the inequality among criminals Furman v. Georgia, 408 U.S. 238, 92 S. Ct. 2726, 33 L. Ed. 2d 346 (1972).

c.   **Brach v. Texas Case Analysis**

A petitioner, Crampton was sentenced to jail for murdering his wife in the court of Ohio. The jury determines if a criminal should live or die. In the case of Crampton, in accordance with the law of Ohio's court, the jury determined punishment and guilt for Crampton after only one trial and verdict. The United States Supreme Court had granted certiorari to review the case, which had been brought by McGautha ALA Schechter Poultry Corp. v. The United States, 295 U.S. 495, 55 S. Ct. 837, 79 L. Ed.

1570 (1935). This petitioner requested the jury that the high court should focus on the constitutional decision of a single verdict and punishment. Procedures of unusual punishment and verdict have violated the fifth and fourteen amendments. The decision based on the single verdict was a part of Illinois's law by accident. One it should be made more apparent that the accused is responsible for the death of another individual or not in a physical sense nor moral Plair v. EJ Brach & Sons, Inc., 105 F.3d 343 (7th Cir. 1997).

Only after considering this accusation, a decision for the death penalty should be made for the defendant should be constitutional or appropriate to impose punishment or not. The absence of basic standards of law to guide the discretion of the jury on the issue of punishment is not tolerable constitutionally. The decision of death penalty on a single verdict and punishment violates the critical command of the fourteen amendments, which states that no state or jury shall decide to sentence someone to the death penalty without following a complete procedure of law Roller v. Holly, 176 U.S. 398, 20 S. Ct. 410, 44 L. Ed. 520 (1900).

d.   McClesky v. Kemp Case Analysis

The petitioner Jackson was also convicted of rape like in the case of Branch. Jackson was an African male who entered into the house of a woman and committed a robbery as well as a rape. During his trial, a psychiatrist confirmed that Jackson was competent and is not schizophrenic and could stand trial when he was not able to stand the trial McCleskey v. Kemp, 481 U.S. 279,

107 S. Ct. 1756, 95 L. Ed. 2d 262 (1987). The Supreme Court of Georgia used reasoning and said that the unequal imposition of the death penalty is not constitutional and also said that the unequal imposition of the death penalty with an existence of some prejudices had been unconstitutional in case of Jackson (Garland, 2017).

The fourteen amendment's law did not mandate the jury for imposing the death penalty and the jury was not given any particular criteria for making death penalty decisions for all the citizens McCleskey v. Kemp, 481 U.S. 279, 107 S. Ct. 1756, 95 L. Ed. 2d 262 (1987). In Jackson's case, nine justices wrote their individual opinion to articulate the reasoning, whereas, five judges voted to reverse the death penalty. The concurring opinions of the juries indicated a shaky decision. Some other judges of the Court of Georgia also doubted that penalty by death was an unusual punishment and is cruel McCleskey v. Kemp, 753 F.2d 877 (11th Cir. 1985). The State of Georgia should make useful guidelines for the juries. Once a criminal is convicted for a crime in a trial, the jury of the court should determine in the severity of a penalty before making the decision to impose a penalty of death (Bohm, 2016).

Race and Death Penalty

Researchers determined that some decisions regarding the death penalty occurred because of racial discrimination that continues to be at the forefront of debate in America (Mauer & Nellis, 2016). Various statistical studies have indicated that race plays a key and decisive role in the life and death of the citizens by execution in the nation. Race contributes towards influencing the choice of different cases for the prosecution and influences the decision of the death penalty by prosecutors (CPC, 2018). Disparities based on race have not only shown in the isolated circumstances but also shown in a number of state studies (Curtin et al., 2016).

Research indicates when the defendant's race has been added to the research analysis, the following pattern arises, 22 percent of the black men who killed white men are convicted to death penalty, only 8 percent of the white men who killed black men receive a death penalty sentence, 1 percent of black men that kill other black me receive the death penalty (Mauer & Nellis, 2016). Results of the analysis indicated that only 64 of 2500 criminal cases studied involved murders of the black man by a white man. Therefore, only 3 percent contributed towards representing the two death penalties over six years (CPC, 2018).

The figures indicated only racial discrimination factors explain these patterns of race. The multiple regression analysis indicated the black man who murdered the white victims was convicted to the death penalty almost 4.3 times more than the white man who killed a black man. The victims' race proves to be a useful predictor of death penalty convictions as the more pressing circumstances in the courts of Georgia (Curtin et al., 2016). On the other hand, the research indicated that only five percent of the Georgia murder resulted in the death penalty whereas, more than

230 non-racial factors that are controlled, the rate for death sentence is almost six percent higher in the cases of white victims than in the cases of black victims (CPC, 2018).

A research study published in the Santa Clara Law Review indicated that the victim's race in the murder cases had been significantly affected by the death sentence of the murderer (DPI, 2018). The study results determined there are more African American or Hispanic victims of murder cases in America as shown in the figure below.

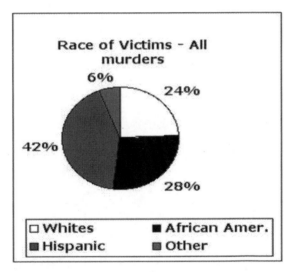

Figure 4: Race of Victim – All murders (Curtin, Warner, & Hedegaard, 2016)

On the other hand, in the cases of the death penalty, there are several cases for white victims than the cases of Hispanic and white American victims (DPI, 2018). The same results have been shown in the figure below:

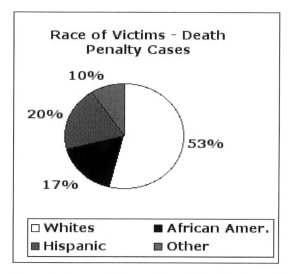

*Figure 5: Race of Victim –Death Penalty Cases (Curtin, Warner, &
Hedegaard, 2016)*

Hence, the conclusions of the research study indicated that
more Hispanics and African American are victims of killings in
America but receive the death penalty at a higher rate for killing
white victims (Mauer & Nellis, 2016).

Alternatives to The Death Penalty

It is found from the conventional wisdom that Americans
support the death penalty. People prefer alternative sentences
instead of the death penalty. The reports provide information that
punishment and protection are both guaranteed in the death penalty
(Daly & Wilson, 2017). There are several alternative sentences
presented and supported by the death penalty to generate awareness
and assist the public. However, most of the people are not entirely
aware of the imprisonment length and the alternative norms applied

by the country. It is to achieve "live without the death penalty" without getting failure in the execution of legal activities (Roberts, 2018).

Since 1976, there is frustration found in the opponents and proponents in America due to the death penalty, while, experiments resulted in a delay to plague, costs, and innocent defendants in the country concerning death punishment (Daly & Wilson, 2017). The outcome of the survey demonstrated that certain stringent sanctions that Americans are willing to enforce due to the death penalty. Alternative sentences to the death penalty are suitable for the compensating victim's family and assure lengthy incarceration (Pratt, 2018).

Because of civil liberties, there must be a constitutional ban against the death penalty as the alternatives are assisting in equal protection and law to guarantee punishment for unfair and unusual acts. In addition, the alternative to the death penalty is capital punishment that allows people discriminatory and arbitrary fashion (McCafferty, 2017). However, capital punishment is considered as an inconsistent and intolerable element that particularly does not address the value of the democratic system fundamentally. The practices of the death penalty are inequitable and unfair for civilized theory. In this regard, capital punishment is the process to prevent and strive legislation, litigation, and advocacy in the brutal and barbaric institution (Daly & Wilson, 2017).

Meanwhile, there are several fundamental concerns incorporated with capital punishment, and includes injustice and unfair support to the people against the race of the victim. It can be said that Caucasians are likely to get an advantage of the US death penalty system. Furthermore, public safety and taxpayer funds are wasted on the death penalty (McCafferty, 2017). Majority of the people consider public safety is in risk because of capital punishment; however, it reduces with the consideration of the death penalty. The death penalty is considered as the practical and suitable way to reduce violence in the country and is known to change things such as reducing drug abuse, increasing the rank of police officers, and creates better options to improve the economy (Tilly, 2017).

Furthermore, sentencing criminals to death is released for innocence to reduce crime and penalty. This reveals that there are two alternatives to the death penalty, which are known as capital punishment and sentenced to death, while capital punishment is considered supportive but not sufficient to provide justice (Daly & Wilson, 2017). Meanwhile, sentenced to death has increased the number of death but the death penalty has controlled the rate of violence in the US and is considered a right and suitable approach to deal with crime (Tilly, 2017).

Chapter Summary

In conclusion, it is found that the death penalty is also termed as capital execution and is when the state or government executes someone for a severe criminal charge. The death penalty is sentenced to people who have committed a serious crime. A crime that can subject individuals with the death penalty is termed as a capital offense or capital crime. Death and executions penalty in the United States was recorded at low levels in 2017. The public support for the death penalty in the US decreased. Per the report released by the US DPIC, the eight states attempted 23 executions that are half the number of previous seven years. Across the US, the political spectrum revealed that more people strive to understand better procedures for offenders than the death penalty. The death penalty since 1990 indicates that in the US the death penalty is becoming obsolete. The condition and statistics are presenting a change in the ratio of death and the leading causes behind the occurrence of the events in the US. The criminal justice system is fair enough that certainly be considered of various countries implementing the death penalty in the state. The death penalty is implicated overwhelmingly in the case of the working class, marginalized groups, and ethnic minorities. The death penalty is the legal way to provide people their rights in case of any misfortune.

References

Bohm, R. M. (2016). Deathquest: An introduction to the theory and practice of capital punishment in the United States. Routledge.

CPC. Capital Punishment Context. Org. (2018). Race and the Death Penalty. Online-link: https://capitalpunishmentincontext.org/issues/race

Curtin, S. C., Warner, M., & Hedegaard, H. (2016). Increase in suicide in the United States, 1999-2014.

Daly, M., & Wilson, M. (2017). Homicide: Foundations of human behavior. Routledge.

Dekker, S. (2017). The field guide to human error investigations. Routledge.

DPI. Death Penalty Info (2018) Race and The Death Penalty In California. Online-Link: https://deathpenaltyinfo.org/node/1534

Fareed, A., Buchanan-Cummings, A. M., Crampton, K., Grant, A., & Drexler, K. (2015). Reversal of overdose on fentanyl being illicitly sold as heroin with naloxone nasal spray: a case report. The American journal on addictions, 24(5), 388-390.

Garland, D. (2017). The Concept of American Exceptionalism and the Case of Capital Punishment. American Exceptionalism in Crime and Punishment, 103.

Gross-Manos, D., Haas, B. M., Richter, F., Crampton, D., Korbin, J. E., Coulton, C. J., & Spilsbury, J. C. (2018). Two sides of the same neighborhood? Multilevel analysis of residents' and child-welfare workers' perspectives on neighborhood social disorder and collective efficacy. The American journal of orthopsychiatry.

Hood, R., & Hoyle, C. (2015). The death penalty: A worldwide perspective. OUP Oxford.

James, W., &Cossman, J. S. (2017). Long-Term Trends in Black and White Mortality in the Rural United States: Evidence of a Race-Specific Rural Mortality Penalty. The Journal of Rural Health, 33(1), 21-31.

Kastellec, J. P. (2016). Race, Context and Judging on the Courts of Appeals: Race-Based Panel Effects in Death Penalty Cases.

Mauer, M. A. R. C., & Nellis, A. S. H. L. E. Y. (2016). The impact of life imprisonment on criminal justice reform in the United States. Life imprisonment and human rights, 23-42.

McCafferty, J. A. (2017). Capital punishment. Routledge.

Morone, J. A., &Kersh, R. (2016). By the people: Debating American government. Oxford University Press.

Pratt, T. C. (2018). Addicted to incarceration: Corrections policy and the politics of misinformation in the United States. Sage Publications.

Reckless, W. C. (2017). The use of the death penalty: a factual statement. In Capital Punishment (pp. 38-62). Routledge.

Roberts, J. (2018). Public opinion, crime, and criminal justice. Routledge.

Shirley, K. E., &Gelman, A. (2015). Hierarchical models for estimating state and demographic trends in US death penalty public opinion. Journal of the Royal Statistical Society: Series A (Statistics in Society), 178(1), 1-28.

Simon, J. (2017). Governing through crime. In Law and Poverty (pp. 97-115). Routledge.

Steiker, C. S., &Steiker, J. M. (2015).The American death penalty and the (in) visibility of race. The University of Chicago Law Review, 243-294.

Tilly, C. (2017). From mobilization to revolution. In Collective Violence, Contentious Politics, and Social Change (pp. 71-91). Routledge.

Toth, Z. J. (2016). The right to life and human dignity in hungary concerning the issue of capital punishment. Constitutional Values in Contemporary Legal Space I, 520.

Zalman, M. (2016). Book Review: Imprisoned by the past: Warren McCleskey and the American death penalty.

CHAPTER SIX

SMART IN OAKLAND AND MINNEAPOLLS DOMESTIC VIOLENCE PROGRAM

SMART (Specialized Multi-Agency Response Team) Program

Introduction and Program Goals

Specialized Multi-Agency Response Team (SMART) program is designed to improve habitation and reduce the problems related to drugs by focusing on the conditions of targeted sites. Research conducted on the evaluation of the topic revealed that the program is effective. In addition, the sites of treatment where this program is applied in the field of arrests or contacts has improved (Moore & Likarish, 2015). Furthermore, the number of arrests with the assistance of the SMART site decreased. The reduction is also evident in the number of a person displayed in the area of addressed catchment and diffusion in the number of new attracted individuals (Peters & Cohen, 2017). The program is designed for teams and it is a team-based program used by the agencies to reduce the problems related to drugs and improve areas with a history of drugs (Moore & Likarish, 2015).

Based on the emergency calls to the police for targeted sites the Oakland Beat Health program was designed for the area to assist police in finding narcotics, make arrests, and engage with, community-based groups or special requests. It is found that the sites could be commercial or residential and experience problems more often from prostitution and blight because of squatters (Curnin et al., 2015). Police use to identify the site and visit it after finding and meeting the shareholders like landlords, community representatives, and business owners to build a working relationship with them (Matheson-Monnet & Jennings, 2017). In the meeting, police explained the purpose of meeting the stakeholder, which is basically to clean-up the area entirely. In addition, the purpose is to bring peace and an effective implementation of rules and regulations for making others safe and secure. After the meeting, the measures of crime prevention were suggested by the police to explain the tenants and rights responsibilities (Kapucu & Haupt, 2016).

It is found that the activities could be different on the basis of site to state the problem-solving tactics and alternatives, and traditional law enforcement methods like posting signs "no trespassing", inspecting the properties of drug-nuisance, increasing the number of sites or police patrols targeted and drug dealers arrest (Matheson-Monnet & Jennings, 2017).

At some time, the considered measures become ineffective and do not lead to improvement in the conditions within a particular area than several regulatory rules and civil laws applied to identify

120

the violations and deployment of SMART (Moore & Likarish, 2015). The representatives of the team can include different agencies including public work, housing, vector control, fire, and public utilities. The representatives inspect the local properties at the time of violations for public work, housing, local fire, public utilities, vector control, and the citation issues of inspectors (Matheson-Monnet & Jennings, 2017). The application of SMART states that the essential citation is associated with the violation of the housing code. It is evident that the resolution of the program matters for the service provider and if it seems ineffective and lacks the capability of rectifying violations then civil laws are applied to bring out drug nuisance against the owner of the properties. The cases of SMART decreased in California and can be rectified by applying the strategies against the property owner through formal court action (Kapucu & Haupt, 2016).

The landlord-training program is a part of the SMART program and aids with informing potential screen renters to encourage landlords. Property owners learn processes for finding the unsatisfactory tenants that can be a problem in particular areas. The fundamental goal of the program is to improve the conditions of society by reducing the consumption of drugs to work on finding drug selling locations (Menete et al., 2017). The inspection of the area is the main problem for the police and other involved authorities. Meanwhile, the capabilities of laws are applied if the processing is not sufficient (Kapucu & Haupt, 2016).

Analyzing SMART and Its Activities

The goal of SMART is to formalize a team-based approach that is effective in improving problems related to drugs and improvement in the conditions of habitation on the sites targeted (Moore & Likarish, 2015).

There are several SMART activities conducted, for instance, Brown, O'Neill, & Yoon (2017), in a study presented that the fields or treatment sites where SMART is being performed experienced improvements. 45.8 is the percentage of arrest or contact, while 13% of the sites were deemed worse. In addition, improvement in the areas of the catchment is increased and now is 75%, the arrest and contact rates roughly recorded at 66 sites are 20%t and growing which is making the situation worse. However, there are several sites recorded as 40% surrounded with the area, largest site, and showing improvements (Matheson-Monnet & Jennings, 2017). There is a significant relationship found at the largest site statistically the border of the surrounding area. The connection of the efforts made by police states success in the overall spilling on the most significant sites affected into the area of boundary to state the benefits of diffusion. The investigation and evaluation revealed that sometimes the situation becomes worse in certain areas (Brown et al., 2017).

Number of People Arrested or Contacted

The decrease in the number of people contacted is significant on all the sites where SMART is applied. From 2014-2018, the rate of reduction increased, and the implementation strategy improved the dimensions of catchment areas that showcase displaced persons to 35%. The attracted new individuals are getting the benefits of SMART implementation and diffusion (Lab, 2018).

Study

A quasi-experimental investigation was conducted to assess and compare the reduction of crime. The results of the experiment indicated the areas of crime and identified that benefited the displacement of other areas. The investigation occurred in 1991, the sample used in the experiment was 321 and the intervention revealed several of problems occurring on the site (Paton & Johnston, 2017). Majority of the sample included residents of the area and the remaining were associated with the property in the area whether rented or leased. The value of the targeted properties was $1 million through other indicated values in the Oakland (Peters & Cohen, 2017).

Information collected from the Department of Oakland Police identified the field contacts and arrests to deal with the problem location. The areas of catchment at SMART sites during the period of contacts and arrests were 70,783 accounted for by 22,335 people (Paton & Johnston, 2017). In the experimental process, before the stated interventions, there were 34 fields and 38 arrests contacted during the year. Displacement was captured for the implementation of ṢMART causing a diffusion of effects and a two-block boundary that delineated the site. A crime mapping software was used by Green to measure the mobility patterns and offenders baseline levels through the computerized investigation (Davis, 2016).

The analysis was based on two-stages a) the overall rate was assessed in the first areas of the catchment to indicate a change in the area for starting SMART implementation and b) the number of means was assessed for arrested/contacted people at the locations of SMART to point out catchment areas. Diffusion effects and displacements were assessed to state the points of sequence and tracking time for field contact and arresting the moving people in the identified areas (Paton & Johnston, 2017).

Evaluating SMART

SMART is a practical approach to develop the policies for improving and habitation conditions. There is a need to identify the area or place that contains a problem or issue to be rectified. However, the strategies are designed by taking the stakeholders into confidence (Peters & Cohen, 2017). SMART allows making people understand the issue and the method of dealing with the issue. The combination of policing with the stakeholder occurs through meetings and discussions occur to find a better way of handling situations. The inspection of the area is the main problem for the police and other involved authorities. Meanwhile, the capabilities of laws are applied if processing is not sufficient (Matheson-Monnet & Jennings, 2017).

The activities of SMART expresses that the essential reference is related to the infringement of the logging code. The goals of the program matter for the specialist organization. The instances of SMART are lower in California and tends to be amended through applying the techniques against the property proprietor through formal court activity (Brown et al., 2017).

It is discovered that the exercises could be distinctive to express the critical thinking strategies and choices and customary law requirement techniques like posting signs "no trespassing", examining the properties of medication irritation, increment in the number of locales, or police watches focused on street pharmacists (Curnin et al., 2015). The object is to bring harmony and compelling the usage of tenets and guideline for making others protected and secure. After this gathering, the proportions of wrongdoing counteractive actions are recommended by the police to clarify the inhabitants and rights duties (Paton & Johnston, 2017).

Policing and SMART

The main aim of policing is to enhance the interaction of the community with the members of public and local agencies to create strategies and partnerships to reduce the disorder and crime. The target of policing is based on several different techniques that deal with the disorder and low-crime level to propose theories and reduce the impact of high efficiency-oriented crime on well-being (Davis, 2016).

In general, community policing is a term that is associated with intelligence-led policing and problem-oriented policing found in the 2oth century and known as reactive policing strategies. The reactive policing eliminates the need of the latter to prevent the issues and make the policing strategies successful (Paton & Johnston, 2017). Several police forces focused on the strategies of community policing strategies and included centralized emergencies and teams of neighborhood policing. SMART is associated with these strategies of the community serving to enhance the effectiveness of security and reduce the ratio of crime from the community (Peters & Cohen, 2017).

The orientation of the drug control program was placed initially in the Oakland Police Department in 1988 to rely on the multiagency task forces associated with the coordination of police for decreasing the problems related to drugs. The condition of targeted sites was improved with the implementation of this strategy (Kapucu & Haupt, 2016). However, the representatives of the agency in the city formed teams to encounter the coerced landowners, nuisance properties, posting signs of no trespassing, municipal regulations, and civil law codes. The civil law citations emphasized the improvement of city conditions (Lab, 2018). Alternative techniques employed by the SMART program was to target the enforcement of traditional drug law that was used for homes, businesses, and rental properties. The dealing of arresting methods was a part of finding the drug problem sites, which stated the significance of drug related activities. These types of problems are a benefit to the area, which led to improving the patterns of programs examined (Peters & Cohen, 2017).

Minneapolis Domestic Violence Program

In the US savagery that occurs at a local dimension is known as aggressive behavior at home, despite the fact that, local dimension pursues the setting of personal relationships among the accomplices (Macy, 2015). The administration and non-government offices remember it as a critical social issue that is related to violence against ladies' acts and exertion to stem the tide by the US Congress. It is discovered that progressing cozy fear-based oppression is expanding to make things increasingly convoluted and crazy regarding misuse and power that endeavors for precise control (Arnold, 2017).

The structure of MDVP depended on gathering arbitrary officers associated with capture procedures directed independently. There were impediment impacts found in consequence of led examinations, which prompted change on the contemporary practices of police (Dasgupta & Pacheco, 2018). There are various law implementation offices ordered to review abusive behavior in home cases and compulsory capture without a warrant and there is a particular reason to capture the general population by the police, which is an event of wrongdoing. Familiarity with the issue began with the frequency and insights of abusive behavior at home for producing activism about the issue in the general population (Macy et al., 2015). In 1976, the information was distributed, and police mediations were established to state promotion to bunch confronting aggressive behavior at home. The mediation procedures were changed and altered to show the help of lawful activity in the gatherings ,which took an interest and incorporated New York City and Oakland for finishing and dragging out the instances of captures causing aggressive behavior at home (Arnold, 2017). In this circumstance, less consideration was paid to the residential unsettling influence calls asserted by the police. The self-governance of the methodology turned into an indication of the proposal for officers to stop the instances of abusive behavior at home. The decrease in the wrongdoing was seen with the usage and reception of the system (Dasgupta, & Pacheco, 2018).

Domestic Violence in the US and Statistics

In the US, violence that occurs at the domestic level is known as domestic violence, although, it follows the context of intimate relationships among partners, against a child, and household violence such as violence between siblings that is also a type of household. The government and non-government agencies recognized it as a critical social problem associated with violence against women acts and efforts to stem the tide by the US Congress (Buzawa & Buzawa, 2017).

Intimate Partners

The boundaries of sexual orientation and gender are transcended in the victimization of domestic violence. Researchers found a high percentage of women victimized through domestic violence as men are found involved in the activities of hurting women physically, but there are some cases recorded in which men are the subject of domestic violence (Trevena & Poynton, 2016). The percentage of domestic violence issues is significantly high for LGBT couples. The issue results in disadvantages for the US government economically and socially; for instance, the percentage of physical assault is 60 percent for the partner (Straus et al., 2017). In addition, several scholarly studies were conducted to find the dynamics of domestic violence and oppression controlled by the relationships. The physical, non-physical, and a multiple of other types of abuse are regularly involved in stating the problem concurrently. Researchers determined the ongoing intimate terrorism is increasing and making things more complicated and out of control based on abuse and power (Buzawa & Buzawa, 2017).

In the US, the average number of physical abuse is 20 people in a minute by intimidating a partner. More than 10 million men and women deal with physical abuse during a year. The ratio of intimate-partner physical violence is 1 out of 4 women and 1 out of 9 men that deal with sexual violence, which causes fearfulness, injury, use of services by the victim, post-traumatic stress disorder, sexually transmitted diseases, and many others issues. The correlation of domestic violence for is high as compared to the other problems (Straus et al., 2017).

Rape

The rate of rape is high in the United States and is one of the main challenges occurring in the domestic violence category. One and 5 women have a history of rape and out of every 71 men, one is associated with rape. This indicates the acquisition of females and males becoming victims of rape, as 46.7% of females and 44.9% of males are raped in the US (Serrata et al., 2017).

Stalking

In the United States, 5.1 million men and 19.3 million women have experience stalking. The current situation indicates that the percentage of women stalked is 60.8% and the percentage of men is 43.5% (Macy et al., 2015).

Homicide

Results from a study conducted on homicide revealed that 20% of the victims in the US due to the intimate partners, friends, family members and found by persons who intervened such as neighbors, bystanders or law enforcement respondents (Dasgupta & Pacheco, 2018).

Children and Domestic Violence

The rate of children and violence is evident in the U S with the rate being explained as 1 out of 15 children is going through violence and the percentage of children that witnessed violence is 90% (Straus et al., 2017).

MDVP Analysis

Minneapolis Domestic Violence Experiment (MDVE) evaluated the effectiveness of different domestic violence responses to police calls in Minneapolis, Minnesota. Lawrence W. Sherman implemented the experiment in 1981-82 with the support of the National Institute of Justice and with the assistance of the Minneapolis Police Department to identify the offenders of domestic violence and the probable causes behind the problem and arrest (Straus et al., 2017). The design of the MDVP study was based on reviewing random officers who were involved in the arrest process. There were deterrent effects found in the result of a conducted investigation, which led to change the impact of unprecedented practices of police (Serrata et al., 2017). There were several law enforcement agencies and states subsequently enacted to the policies of domestic violence cases, mandatory arrest without any warrant; however, there was specific cause to arrest the people (Danis, 2016).

In the experiment, the history of domestic violence was viewed while attention was given to the private matters of the family and the involvement of criminal justice intervention and government was avoided. In the 1970s, police in the US developed a hands-off approach was implemented by police to end domestic violence and arresting suspects was the last resort (Leisenring, 2016). It is identified that the cases of domestic violence were classified and treated as a misdemeanor assault. However, the jurisdiction of US authority and the police identified occurrences and determined issues to make arrests. The order of arrest was taken seriously in 1978 when the dispute of families started becoming mediate (Griffin, 2018).

Awareness of the problem was originated with the incidence and statistics of domestic violence for generating activism about the problem in public. In 1976, the data was published, and police interventions were founded to state advocacy to groups facing domestic violence (Danis, 2016). The intervention strategies were changed and modified seriously to indicate the assistance of legal action to the groups such as New York City and Oakland for completing and prolonging the cases of arrests causing domestic violence. In this situation, less attention was paid to the domestic disturbance calls claimed by the police (Leisenring, 2016).

The National Academy of Science published a report in 1978, which was associated to the practices and policies that were more rigorous and stated the use of crime and social control theories. Recommendations about the academy was provided to begin funding studies by the National Institute of Justice on the effects of deterrent regarding the sanctions described as criminal sanctions.

The outcomes of the analysis are associated with the methods used in the experiment; however, attention was given to use the services of police for reducing domestic violence. Call for service was the phenomenon followed by calls made by the victims of domestic violence against the offenders (Pinchevsky, 2017). The number of participants was 51 and participants were patrol officers. The process followed was explained as making a call, sending the abusers on any other location for a specific duration, mediation, and advice of disputes and arrest (Leisenring, 2016).

In most of the responses from a police arrest was found, the outcomes of the investigation revealed that offenders must be arrested to decrease the rate of reoffending and the offenders must be sent away to a new location (Xie & Lynch, 2017).

Police Response and Arrest Policies

The experiment received massive attention from the media including prime time news and The New York Times. Responses of different police departments of the UK was recorded, and the arrest policy was adopted, which made it mandatory for dealing with spoUSl violence cases in the US. Benjamin Ward issued a new mandate to read the outcomes of the investigation and make immediate arrest in the report of police foundation (Leisenring, 2016). The results of the experiment indicated that the policy is sufficient to protect people and family members from domestic violence with the help of police officers. At that time, the process seemed like law enforcement officers have started the business of counseling. However, a judge decided on the arrests based on a mandate (Dempsey, 2016).

In addition to this, during the 1980s and 90s arrest laws were implemented and became mandatory to be implemented by the police in the US to extend the influence of the Minneapolis Experiment. In 1994, the Violence Against Women Act was presented based on the legislation to add value into the pertaining of laws to make the arrest a necessary part of the law (Prenzler & Fardell, 2017). This could affect the states and laws, but it is required to indicate and present the probable reasons behind police arrest in domestic violence cases. There was a high influence of the law on the victims and police to reduce the consequences of arrest as well as to overcome the occurrence of abuse at large. Decisions were made about the discretion of arrest for the officers to give their response (Raymond et al., 2016). Research found that a high number of police officers developed the policies and approaches after the success of the experiment. The autonomy of the approach became a sign of recommendation for officers to overcome cases of domestic violence. Crime reduction occurred with the implementation and adoption of the technique (Fraser, 2017).

Evaluation and Criticism

The investigation on domestic violence indicated that in some states arrest are made based on probable cause. However, some use this act on specific incidents were evident and logical. For instance, police in Alaska made an arrest after recording 12 hours of abuse (Pinchevsky, 2017). The notification provided information about the act and police assessed the situation correctly for training, deciding probable cause required for making an arrest (Raymond et al., 2016). In addition to this, a list of requirements was developed before making an arrest by the officer and includes, relationship with the victim, age, and analysis of the act as either an intentional assault or not. It is stated that the predominant aggressor is needed to be identified in this situation (Holt, 2016).

In the US, consistent research was conducted on the issues of domestic violence, which resulted in increased arrests. However, the study regarding the representatives stemmed from 650,000 incidents in the year 2000 in 19 states from 2.810 jurisdictions (Macy et al., 2015). From the results of the studies, the police arrested 48 percent of people in the cases and dual arrest made in 1.9 percent of the total cases. This includes the cases of domestic violence for heterosexual couples and same-sex relationships and stated that offenders are likely to arrest the partner if assault was suspected (Dasgupta & Pacheco, 2018).

Research found that intimate partners are frequently involved in the occurrence of arrest reported for NIJ in the case of acquaintances in the partners, as one of the involved partners in the cases was white. Police are more likely to arrest the partner or offender in result if older than 21. It was a huge concern for the community had increased the number of arrests of both males and females. The incidents of dual arrest increased consequences for the approach (Buzawa & Buzawa, 2017).

In this regard, the conclusions and methods of the Minneapolis Experiment were criticized, and six months was used for follow up to capture the accurate picture and to reduce the cyclical patterns of domestic violence (Trevena & Poynton, 2016). The outcomes were not usual for Minneapolis and arrests were made while, the release of the arrests was quicker for the jurisdiction's arrestees. This was a tragedy factor and increased criticism on the method of arrest (Straus et al., 2017).

The methodological strength of the Minneapolis design was integrated to review the average caUSl effects of randomized experiments for the entire group. Based on individual applications, conclusions can be made about the group that was not suitable for all the individuals (Macy et al., 2015). Adverse effects were possibly experienced and intervened because of the experiment. In addition to this, some of the domestic violence cases provoked arrest and increased the possibility of high revengeful violence by the abuser. This indicates that threats to the individual increased due to the application of the experiment (Straus et al., 2017).

The deterrence theory was applied in the Minneapolis Experiment that was based on the assumptions of rational decision making by the offenders. Domestic violence was the original case or focus of attention. There was little rational behavior often found from the side of offenders (Serrata et al., 2017). Furthermore, the measures of the Minneapolis Experiment indicated crucial elements of deterrence theory that were increasing the number of arrests for the offenders (Macy et al., 2015).

Chapter Summary

The SMART program is intended to improve law and decrease the issues identified by concentrating on focused locations and areas. Research led the assessment of the subject and uncovered that the program is viable. In addition, the locales of the treatment program are connected in the field of captures or contacts experienced enhancements. Besides, the quantity of captures is decreased with the help of the SMART site. The decrease is evident in the quantity of individuals showed in the territory of dissemination. The program was intended to be drawn closer by the group-based program utilized by the offices to diminish the issues identified with medication and improvement in the states of residence identified. Police use to recognize the site and visit it in the wake of finding and meeting investors like landowners, network agents, and entrepreneurs.

In the US savagery happens at social dimension is known as aggressive behavior at home, despite the fact that it pursues the setting of the special relationship among the accomplices that states family unit viciousness. The legislature and non-government organizations remember it as a critical social issue related to violence against women acts and exertion to stem the tide by the US Congress.

The limits of sexual introduction and sex rises above the exploitation of aggressive behavior at home. It is discovered that the level of women is high for aggressive behavior at home and unfortunate casualties such as men are discovered engaged with the exercises of harming women physically; however, there are a few cases recorded in which men are the subject of abusive behavior. The level of abusive behavior at home issues is fundamentally high for LGBT couples. In the vast majority of the reactions of police, the capture was discovered, the results of the examination uncovered that wrongdoers must be captured to diminish the rate of reoffending and the guilty parties must be sent away or on another area for directing incidentally.

References

Arnold, G. (2017). US women's movements to end violence against women, domestic abuse, and rape. *The Oxford handbook of US women's social movement activism*, 270.

Brown, A. T., O'Neill, O. M., & Yoon, K. Y. (2017). Cluster coordination in a government-led emergency response in Ethiopia. Field Exchange 56, 20.

Buzawa, E. S., & Buzawa, C. G. (2017). The evolution of the response to domestic violence in the United States. In *Global Responses to Domestic Violence* (pp. 61-86). Springer, Cham.

Curnin, S., Owen, C., Paton, D., Trist, C., & Parsons, D. (2015). Role clarity, swift trust and multi-agency coordination. Journal of Contingencies and Crisis Management, 23(1), 29-35.

Danis, F. S. (2016). Teaching domestic violence online: a step forward or a step backward?. *Violence against women, 22*(12), 1476-1483.

Dasgupta, K., & Pacheco, G. (2018). Warrantless arrest laws for domestic violence: How are youth affected?. *The BE Journal of Economic Analysis & Policy, 18*(1).

Davis, M. (2016). Law enforcement response to intimate partner sexual violence perpetrators. Perpetrators of Intimate Partner Sexual Violence: A Multidisciplinary Approach to Prevention, Recognition, and Intervention, 206.

Dempsey, M. (2016). Domestic violence and the United States' criminal justice system. *Changing Contours of Criminal Justice*, 243.

Fraser, J. (2017). Making Domestic Violence a Crime: Situating the Criminal Justice Response in Canada. In *Global Responses to Domestic Violence* (pp. 41-59). Springer, Cham.

Griffin, J. (2018). *A State Report Card: Evaluation of Domestic Violence Victim-Centered Legislation by State* (Doctoral dissertation, Northern Arizona University).

Holt, A. (2016). Adolescent-to-Parent Abuse as a Form of "Domestic Violence" A Conceptual Review. *Trauma, Violence, & Abuse, 17*(5), 490-499.

Kapucu, N., & Haupt, B. (2016). Information communication technology use for public safety in the United States. Frontiers in communication, 1, 8.

Lab, S. P. (2018). Prevention and prevarication: the fits and starts of prevention in the US. Crime Prevention and Community Safety, 1-13.

Leisenring, A. (2016). Intimate Partner Violence, US Criminal Justice Response to. *Encyclopedia of Family Studies*, 1-4.

Macy, R. J., Ogbonnaya, I. N., & Martin, S. L. (2015). Providers' perspectives about helpful information for evaluating domestic violence and sexual assault services: A practice note. *Violence against women, 21*(3), 416-429.

Matheson-Monnet, C. B., & Jennings, P. (2017). A Review of Quality Improvement [QI] Specialised Interventions in the

US and England to Reduce the Number of Police Mental Health Crisis Detentions and Provide Support to High Intensity Utilisers [HIUs]. Open Medicine Journal, 4(1).

Menete, S., Mavee, A., Ehlers, E. M., & Leung, W. S. (2017, July). Smart grid critical information infrasructure protection through multi-agency. In 2017 Computing Conference (pp. 461-468). IEEE.

Moore, E., & Likarish, D. (2015, May). A cyber security multi agency collaboration for rapid response that uses AGILE methods on an education infrastructure. In IFIP World Conference on Information Security Education (pp. 41-50). Springer, Cham.

Paton, D., & Johnston, D. (2017). Disaster resilience: an integrated approach. Charles C Thomas Publisher.

Peters, A. M., & Cohen, I. M. (2017). The mandate and activities of a specialized crime reduction policing unit in Canada. Police Practice and Research, 18(6), 570-583.

Peters, A. M., & Cohen, I. M. (2017). The mandate and activities of a specialized crime reduction policing unit in Canada. Police Practice and Research, 18(6), 570-583.

Pinchevsky, G. M. (2017). Exploring the effects of court dispositions on future domestic violence offending: an analysis of two specialized domestic violence courts. *Journal of interpersonal violence*, *32*(4), 558-580.

Prenzler, T., & Fardell, L. (2017). Situational prevention of domestic violence: A review of security-based programs. *Aggression and violent behavior, 34*, 51-58.

Raymond, J. L., Spencer, R. A., Lynch, A. O., & Clark, C. J. (2016). Building Nehemiah's Wall: The North Minneapolis Faith Community's Role in the Prevention of Intimate Partner Violence. *Violence and victims, 31*(6), 1064-1079.

Serrata, J. V., Macias, R. L., Rosales, A., Hernandez-Martinez, M., Rodriguez, R., & Perilla, J. L. (2017). Expanding evidence-based practice models for domestic violence initiatives: A community-centered approach. *Psychology of violence, 7*(1), 158.

Straus, M. A., Gelles, R. J., & Steinmetz, S. K. (2017). *Behind closed doors: Violence in the American family*. Routledge.

Trevena, J., & Poynton, S. (2016). Does a prison sentence affect future domestic violence reoffending?. *BOCSAR NSW Crime and Justice Bulletins*, 12.

Xie, M., & Lynch, J. P. (2017). The effects of arrest, reporting to the police, and victim services on intimate partner violence. *Journal of research in crime and delinquency, 54*(3), 338-378.

CHAPTER SEVEN
ILLEGAL DRUGS AND THE US CRIMINAL JUSTICE SYSTEM

Introduction

The extent of drug-related crime is not evident and is probably impossible to state and determine the exact number of crimes, but the identification of drug related crime is significant by using several government sources and data accordingly. In the recent records of crime, it is found that victims found the offender in drugs influence less than the actual arrested criminal (Foppe et al., 2018). However, the number of violent crimes for drug related crimes investigated from drugs tests is low. Similarly, the percentage is high for the USge of drugs. In addition, it was found that sometimes drugs are the cause of criminal activity and it is evident in cases when the offender is not found influenced from crime commitment (Oteng-Ababio et al., 2017). In addition, crime is committed by offenders to get money for drugs. If adding all the crimes, causes, and influences on people, some criminal offenses are associated with drugs and a high number of the crimes include illegal possession. Drugs play the role of the agent in the cases extensively (Foppe et al., 2018).

The US Bureau of Justice System collects data for violent crimes from the victims. In addition, victim's perception about the commission of the crime for the offender can be categorized under the following influences such as rapes or sexual assaults (Thomson, 2017). Research found different percentages for crimes such as crimes of violence 24%, assault, 24%, robbery, 23%, simple assault, 25% and robbery 23%. Several cases were monitored to collect information and it was determined that the offenders are increasing due to the increase in substance use and it is essential to limit the use of drugs in particular locations to reduce the rate of crime (Foppe et al., 2018).

The three common types of crimes associated with the use of drugs are as follows.

Use-related crime – the occurrence of the crime is associated with self-ingestion of drugs and results in crime commitment, which affects the behaviors and thought process of the individual (Allen, 2016).

Economic-related crime – these are crimes attempted to fund the habit of the drug through crimes such as prostitution and theft (Brownstein, 2016).

System-related crime – the occurrence of the crime is dependent on the structure of the drug system including transportation, manufacturing, production, and sale of drugs. In

144

addition, this includes the sale and production of drugs for creating violence (Huber Newman & LaFave, 2016).

US statistics revealed that out of 10 children, four are the victims of crimes related to drugs. It is found that the drinkers use to drink alcohol for preceding offenses. The analysis on the use of substance indicated that negligence of parents towards children is increasing addiction and substance abuse, and the percentage is expected to increase in the coming years (Guiney, 2016).

Violence is also increasing due to the use of drugs and the incidents caused by the offenders are becoming familiar to assault the intimate partner. The percentage of physical violence is 33 %, and 16 % of the violence is caused by the use of drugs (Foppe et al., 2018). In addition, family members promote the experience of domestic violence with the use of drugs or alcohol. The chances of abuse are likely to highlight violence around the age group of 18 to 24 causing the use of substances such as drugs and alcohol (Thomson, 2017). Sexual assault and acquaintance rape increased on the campuses of colleges due to the use of drugs. Society is profoundly affected by the use of these substances. The justice system must follow practical steps to overcome this problem (Foppe et al., 2018).

War on Drugs

It has been more than 25 years that the US engaged in a war on drugs and the war caused confusion. It is due to the right reasons for conducting war and engaging the authorities to obtain desirable results. There are various point of views on the subject due to the resolutions and mathematical proofs (Lassiter, 2015). The war is now continuing to become a struggle with a fundamental question that is "war on drugs." Research has been conducted to investigate if the US can win this war or not or it will be harmful to the country and is having substantial medical side-effects (Shannon, 2015). The people addictive to drugs can destroy their life, job, and family. Mainly, drugs are having adverse effects on the life of individuals and for ending these side effects to find a solution irrespective to the cost paid on eradicating the ineffective battle (Lassiter, 2015). Some studies analyzed whether it is possible to end the substance use and showing the positive side of the war. However, the possibility of reducing the harm of substance use is very low. The options for the use of drugs are explained to improve the future of the US (Redford & Powell, 2016).

The country is spending more than $50 billion a year to eradicate the use of drugs. The estimation made by DAE revealed that the percentage of illicit drugs is 10% (Castañeda, 2018). Providing evaluations, analyses, and investigating situations could help with overcoming problems. At times, overcoming problems could cost money on resources without a guarantee of productivity.

The attempts are not adequately under legislative control, thus generating incarcerate for causing deaths of the addictive people (Redford & Powell, 2016). The estimated death of the addictive people per year is 400,000, while finding solutions, these solutions may not help. This has led to severe problems on the inevitable progression of the US (Lassiter, 2015).

The original investigation on the subject matter revealed this increased use and production of drugs caused severe effects and violence in society. The investigation results indicated cases of the people with broken bones in their hands for ripping their hands from handcuffs. The worse thing is those individuals using drugs not understanding their actions; specifically, in cases of crack and cocaine use (Castañeda, 2018). For example, the experimentation of cocaine and an addiction to heroin killed Len Bias, a basketball player. In addition to individuals dying from a drug overdose, AIDS is spreading into society with the proliferation of sharing the needles (Walker, 2015).

The category of severe and addictive drugs is lumped into a final verification of this type of drug use. A scientific study indicated that marijuana does not fit in this category because marijuana s beneficial for medical use in terms of controlling nausea, pain relief, and appetite stimulation (Hari, 2015). The study results indicated marijuana as a gateway drug. However, the war identified the type of drugs that are increasing the rate of crime in the country. In this regard, the directive points regarding marijuana were reconsidered for further evaluation in legislation (Mott, 2018).

Penalties were applied to the people found using and producing these drugs. The results indicated success in prohibiting the use of drugs by applying reformed policies with continued ineffectiveness and costs on the problematic approach (Villa et al., 2016). There were several angles associated with the approach that were adequate to stop drug offenders. Though the programs were applied to provide knowledge, money was spent on the idea decreasing the use of alcohol and cigarettes in schools (Walker, 2015).

Steps were taken to discourage people from using alcohol, cigarettes, and marijuana instead of making usage and possession illegal. Education and support about the war on drugs could help individuals understand which drugs are illegal (Villa et al., 2016). The main points to formalize and outline the problem align with the need for change and keeping the perception that drugs are illegal. The outcomes of the war indicated that it is a failed war and drugs used in the country cannot be illegal (Bergen-Cico, 2015).

However, a considerable amount of money is spent on prisons and law enforcement for drug offenders but death, violence, and disease continue during the war on drug because of newer more potent substances s (Lim, 2018). Civil rights are eroded in order to conduct wiretaps to find criminals. The organizations have become criminal enriched and these criminals become desperate to escape from being captured while police encroach individuals using incentives that ultimately removes protection for criminals (Villa, 2016).

Commonly Used Drugs in US and Explanations

The commonly used drugs in the US are as follows.

Marijuana

It is one of illicit drug used by 27.1 million people and NSDUH has indicated that in a month, almost 22.2 million people use marijuana. The rate of marijuana usage is widely spread in the US and young people are focusing on the illegal use of this drug (Guney et al., 2016). Increase in the consumption of marijuana is a result of the legalization of the drug for medical purposes. The drug is less harmful to young people as compared to other available drugs and on a national average, 74 percent of people are consuming marijuana (Segal et al., 2018).

Psychotherapeutics

The second massive drug-oriented problem for the US should be for medical use but used for non-medical purposes (Hartung et al., 2015). There are four categories of drugs for medical purposes found in the report from NSDUH includes tranquilizers, prescription-type pain relievers, sedatives, and stimulants. The combination of the category is known as "psychotherapeutics."

The survey of NSDUH estimated that in the past 6.4 million people misused psychotherapeutic drugs, the estimation includes the people using it as pain relievers. However, a law enforcement crackdown system or prescription-tracking system must be employed on the "pill mills" to reduce prescription drug addiction growth, as this is a rising concern for the health of the public (Gossop, 2016).

Cocaine

Presently, in America, 1.9 million people are using crack cocaine or cocaine, the consumption of the drug depends on the form. Cocaine could be consumed in several ways like injected, snorted, or even smoked (Segal et al, 2018). In all the cases, the drug is expected to have a substantial impact on the central nervous system, which can affect the brain processing dopamine. Cocaine is found to be powerfully prevalent in the country since the 1980s; however, the consumption of the drug is found to be decreasing due to the segments of society, while for traditional users, it is still popular and available (Meier, 2016).

Hallucinogens

A variety of substances is included in hallucinogens, such as peyote, PCP, mescaline, LSD, mushrooms, psilocybin, and others. It is found that all of the substance is capable of abuse. The investigation on the consumption of Hallucinogens has revealed that in the United States, 1.2 million people are currently using this drug (Gossop, 2016). The probable use of hallucinogens has increased from the 1960s and 1970s and peaked in the hippie movement. Furthermore, there are a considerable number of young people willing to experiment with drugs to get mind-altering effects (Maier et al., 2018).

Ecstasy

The drug falls in the category of hallucinogens included by NSDUH, which is ecstasy. The drug is also known as MDMA due to the formation 3, 4-methylenedioxymethamphetamine (Hartung et al., 2015). Meanwhile, the other common names of the drug are XTC on the street, molly, and contains mind-altering drug, psychoactive, and amphetamine-like properties. Officials have indicated that people attending raves consider this drug as a favorite while it has been encouraged by the societal segments in recent years (Maier et al., 2018).

Methamphetamine

A study conducted by NSDUH in 2015 included categories of drugs available to people through prescriptions; this included the psychotherapeutics category. It is essential to understand and recognize the distribution is legal or illegal yet, it is found that methamphetamine in the category of the survey is illegal (Peters,

2018). The age of the current users of this drug is 12 or older and the estimated number of people using this drug is 897,000 and is made of over the counter medication ingredients. The list of the ingredients includes pose specific health threats, especially crystal methamphetamine, methamphetamine taken intravenously (Hutton et al., 2015). The number of clandestine methamphetamine labs is reduced to counter the illegal production of the medications used forcold and allergy in many states. Meanwhile, the cartels of the international drug have taken part in the continued demand and supply for the drugs considered as highly-addictive (Kantor et al., 2015).

Inhalants

Inhalants are vapors or breathable chemicals that produce psychoactive effects. Young people are often abused by it; however, it is easily accessible and not illegal. It is found that almost 600,000 people are buying the inhalants monthly (Hartung et al., 2015).

Powder vs. Crack Cocaine

The powder of hydrochloride salt is known as salt, whereas, the combination of water, powdered cocaine, and another substance is the composition structure of crack cocaine. Usually, the substance used for the formation is sodium bicarbonate or baking soda, and the solid form achieved by boiling the mixture and combining the components. The blocks and pieces cool down and then broken into small pieces, known as crack (Oliveira et al., 2018). According to the Center for Substance Abuse Research, the derivation of the name is made from the crackling sound produced from the smoked and heated drug. The substance is extremely addictive as it is highly concentrated (Evans et al., 2018).

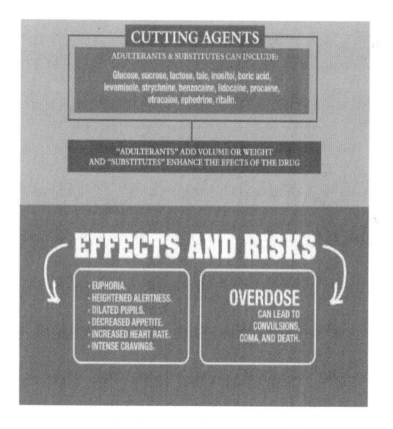

Figure 6: *Explanation of the cutting agents (Oliveira et al., 2018).*

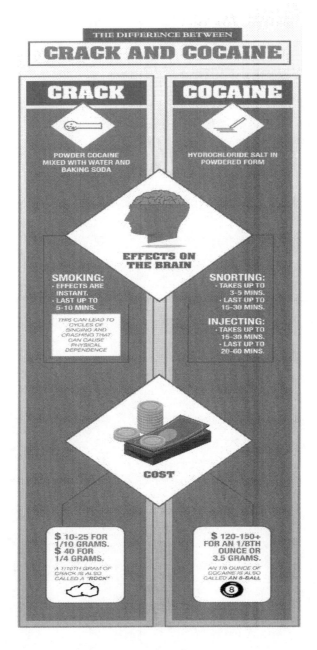

Figure 7: *Difference between crack and cocaine (Evans et., 2018)*

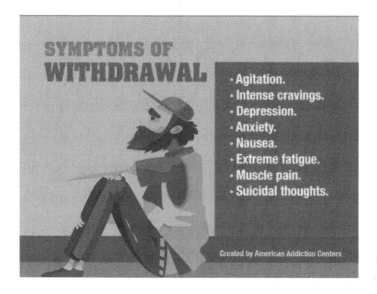

Figure 8: *Symptoms of withdrawal (Oliveira et al. 2018)*

The appearance of crack and cocaine certainly is different from the other. Generally, cocaine is found in powder form white in color and crack in rock form, which could be in a cream, white, light brown or tan. How crack and cocaine are used is also different from each other, as the crack is consumed by smoking and cocaine is used as snorted (Gootenberg, 2015). The production of the substances is also different from each other; however, the National Institute on Drug Abuse stated that the duration and intensity of the substances is highly related to each other. In general, cocaine is injected in the body; thus, the effect is stronger and quicker, which results in profound effects for a short time. Similarly, the effect and feeling of cocaine if snorted stems for a long time (Greer et al., 2016).

The investigation of a clinical pharmacist indicated that the effects of crack and cocaine on the body of a person are different and these effects are primarily associated to the general administration of the substance on the body. If the substance is snorted the reaction takes 1-5 minutes to occur and in between 20 to 30 minutes, it shows high impact which dissipates until 1 or 2 hours (Shimomura et al., 2019). On the other side, the crack starts its effect in just a minute, gets on the peak in 3 to 5 minutes and dissipates between 30 to 60 minutes. Meanwhile, if cocaine is taken through an injection, then the duration and effect will be the same as crack. In addition, the traditional method to consume cocaine is through snorting and not through injection (Evans et al., 2018).

More people use crack because the substance is cheaper than cocaine. Besides, at the lower socioeconomic demographic, it is easily accessible, and the easy affordability increases the number of users (Oliveira et al., 2018). In the early 1980s, crack was an epidemic in the communities, which led to the phenomenon that cocaine is for prosperous drug users, and crack associated with minorities and lower income brackets (Shimomura et al., 2019). The information collected by the National Institute on Drug Abuse indicated that Caucasians are the critical users of crack. The investigation has further stated that there are 1.9 million users of cocaine and the number is including 359,000 users of crack (Malone, 2018).

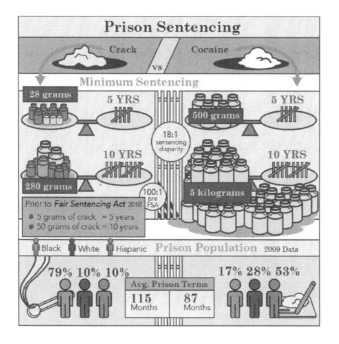

Figure 9: *Prison sentencing (Miró et al. 2019)*

On legal grounds, before 1986, both cocaine and crack were treated as the same with more men being addicted to crack, according to the information provided by Newsweek. The enactment of The Anti-Drug Abuse Act of 1986 developed sentencing for minimum five years due to possession of 5 gm of cocaine as the first offense and minimum five-year sentence for the consumption of 500 grams cocaine. Ratio sentencing began for people on the amount 100 times of cocaine as of crack with the minimum mandatory sentence of five-years (Evans et al., 2018).

The act was considered as "ration sentencing" resulted in the arrest of African Americans caught with at least 5 grams of crack. In this regard, those men started residing in the places where the

157

production of crack was readily available in low prices, particularly in low-income neighborhoods. This increased the epidemic of criminal targets for African Americans. Eighty percent of crack offenses were for the African Americans (Palamar et al., 2015).

In the end, this legal action created social and racial disparity among the people to process and endure legal terms until the passage of the Fair Sentencing Act. The act was presented in the year of 2010 and eliminated the necessary amount of crack used and a minimum sentence of 5 years mandatory for the consumed amount resulted in a minimum sentence (Shimomura et al., 2019). The ratio of crack-to-powder-cocaine was also changed using this Act, though, the amount substituted equal sentence was 100-to-1 to 18-to-1, there is still a disparity in the sentencing which is required to be reduced significantly from 18:1 (Miró et al., 2019).

Rockefeller Drugs Laws and Mass Incarceration

The statutes developed for dealing with the possession and sale of narcotic is known as Rockefeller drug laws applied in the New York State penal law. The law was adopted from the name of "Nelson Rockefeller, who was the state governor and adopted the law" (Green, 2017). Rockefeller backed the rehabilitation of drugs using housing and job training as the strategies. The use of drugs is a criminal and social problem mounting the national anxiety, making the use of the drug as a crime (Engstrom et al., 2017).

Rockefeller supported laws containing the bill because of presidential ambitions as well as working to posture strictness on crime at the national level. The act was signed in 1973 and was stated that the acceptance of the strategy would end the liberality of Rockefeller to be elected for president (Temin, 2017). The law stated penalty of selling different amounts of the drugs with particular consumption causing a sentence of 15 years to life prison. The mandate of the original legislation was the same against violent crimes in the community with the influence of drug use; however, the bill omitted the provision after Rockefeller passed this legislation (Engstrom et al., 2017). The law's section was replaced in 1977 for marijuana by Governor Hugh Carey under the Democratic (Green, 2017).

Meanwhile, the adoption of Rockefeller's drug laws gave the distinction of the most complicated laws in the state of New York. The imitation of the approach was replaced in 1978 by Michigan who controlled a "650 lifer law". This law was known as life imprisonment due to the possible sale of, possession, and manufacturing of 650 grams of cocaine (Spillane, 2016).

The investigation of Nixon's domestic policy found that the campaign was targeting two enemies; mainly, this campaign was treated as antiwar left and black people. The use of drugs is illegal, but it seemed like a war against blacks, the formation of connecting heroin with blacks and marijuana with hippies was disrupting the communities as both substances were heavily criminalized. The law allowed for arresting leaders, breaking meetings, raiding homes, vilifying users daily in the evening news (Pettit & Gutierrez, 2018).

The statues of Michigan and New York faced harsh criticism in terms of political rights and the political left. Mainly, there were some famous people against the enforcement of the law, for instance, William F. Buckley, who is America's most conservative figures. According to him, the enforcement was reflecting the inheritance of unfairness against drug trafficking and non-violent crime par with murder (Fortner, 2016). Ultimately, the program was a fiasco and generated many medical or social problems using the Billy club and jail. The advocates of civil rights showed intense opposition and claimed the law is racist as well as applied onto African Americans inordinately (Harris, 2016).

There were many protests conducted against the law, and individuals believed the implementation of the drug laws was not valid; it increased the incarceration rates since 1973. In New York, there were 150,000 people imprisoned due to the use of drugs and non-violent drug offenses (Pettit & Gutierrez, 2018). There were harsh penalties imposed using the law on the non-violent drug offenses, while, reduction in the number of crime caused by drugs was not reduced. The number of prisoners increased after imposing the law and the condition was expected to get worse. Approximately, 19,164 drug offenses were incarcerated (Fortner, 2016).

The analysis of the laws faced several more criticism, which was needed to be handled and covered through developing new reforms and laws associated with the use of drugs. Thus, the Drug Law Reform Act (DLRA) was applied by George Pataki in the New York to replace the general scheme of sentencing for the determinate system of Rockefeller Drug Laws, the convictions and penalties were reduced by the implementation of the law (Harris, 2016).

There were two serious possession offenses and weight thresholds (A-I and A-II narcotics felonies) causing offenders to serve life sentences that eventually were reduced. More than half of the A-I narcotics felony prison sentences were reduced. The laws of the criminal justice system were discussed to revise mandatory minimum sentences (Temin, 2018). Judicial diversion was applied to convict the offenders and shorten sentences and there was treatment available for drug users as a means to reduce sentences for incarcerated defendants because treatment was essential to make the release of the defendants possible (Pattillo, 2017). Offenders began to accept the new implementation of the law and the reductions in sentencing because the law began to end racism and negativity (Pettit & Gutierrez, 2018).

Drug Courts and Rehabilitation

The first official drug court was instituted in Florida in 1989, with the purpose of integrating treatments for drug users through the criminal justice system. Law enforcement provided information to the nation about the abuse of drugs and strategies to end the epidemic (Murphy, 2015). The abuse problem or drug dependence was evident in 53 percent of the prisons. The courts based on docket programs for the specialized court that is integrated to the offenders and defendants of targeted criminals, parents and juvenile offenders with the cases of child welfare that are pending due to drug, alcohol and other substance dependency problems (Nolan, 2017). The drug courts estimated that the majority of operating courts in US were child welfare, DWI (driving while intoxicated), veterans, and juveniles (Murphy, 2015).

The design of the program was associated with the target population, service resources and comprehension of the model in general terms included; judicial interaction, assessment of needs, risks, responsivity and offender screening, supervision and monitoring, incentives and graduated sanction, rehabilitation, and treatment services (Hueston & Burke, 2016). Courts are designed to manage a multidisciplinary and non-adversarial team that includes prosecutors, judges, community corrections, defense attorneys, treatment service professionals, and social workers (McColl, 2017). Law enforcement gets support from the stakeholders, community, and families through program

162

encouragement and participation in hearings and events (Murphy, 2015).

People get treatment for a long time and earn the chance of traditional sentences, recovery of jail time. The supervision time for most of the cases is considered one year, the minimum time duration designed for the program (Murphy, 2015). The courts aim to offer treatment to the prisoners and users of drugs. The senior judge of America discussed the operation of the program. The judge introduced the program to local judges, people working for the criminal justice system, and politicians (Hueston & Burke, 2016). The prohibition board made it compulsory for the court to analyze the criminal cases effectively; even cases not related to the use of drugs with a few cases underlined with crime caused because of drug use (McColl, 2017).

In addition, there were some offenders found in the possession of cocaine and heroin for personal use and these were the people offered methods such as monitored treatment and long-term rehabilitation programs to escape conviction and prison (Bean, 2017). This strategy indicated that drug courts are not designed to give punishment to the people and the successful completion of the program meant individuals were no longer a part of the criminal justice system. Almost half of the people enrolled completed the program and the courthouses recognized the achievements (Ruiz et al., 2018).

The statistics are impressive because the implementation of the program reduced the occurrence of crime. Besides, the politicians and the public recognized the soft option. However, there is an enormous difference between the aspects of the process and jurisdictions (Hueston & Burke, 2016). The program offers several services and intensive treatment for maintaining recovery and becoming accountable. Offenders receive sentencing and are informed of their obligations to society, the court, and their families (Ruiz et al., 2018). While in the program, users receive monitoring and random drug tests. The overall process is analyzed and available rewards are offered to the offenders if there is progress, if there is no progress an offender earns sanctions (Hueston & Burke, 2016).

The treatment and consideration of drug courts vary, as there are several drug courts with some of courts offering punishments and incentives to the offenders, methods of legal restriction, and community integration; however, this approach is not suitable for all drug courts (Murphy, 2015). Meanwhile, understanding practical and suitable options is investigated from the assessment of the offender. The local guidelines are analyzed as well as an investigation of the functioning and impact of the courts on the neglect/abuse of individuals (Hueston & Burke, 2016).

DARE (Drug Abuse Resistance Education) Program and Analysis

DARE is a program designed for the prevention of drug abuse using the teaching of skills to students for resisting and recognizing the social pressures associated with the use of drugs. In addition, the program offers techniques for coping, self-esteem, communication skills and assertiveness, decision-making skills, risk assessment, and identification of alternatives to drug use by uniformed police (Marsiglia et al., 2018). The police officers provide 17 lessons a week for 50 minutes as wellas extensive training if requested. The duration of the training is 80 hours with a wide range of activities taught such as a session of question and answers using workbook exercises, role play, and group discussion (Thomas et al., 2015).

Dr. Ruth Rich was the one who created this curriculum for the specialists of Los Angeles Unified School District, and it was designed for the elementary schools of Los Angeles as Self-Management and Resistance Training (SMART) (Caputi, & Thomas-McLellan, 2017). Initially, the program was designed for 345 schools but expanded to junior high school. The drug prevention program spread into 80,000 classrooms and over three million children (Thomas et al., 2015). The program is employed to every school health curriculum to adopt the operations of reservation for the schools. Efforts and strategies are developed for improvising teaching methods for DARE to make the process meet the unique needs of children having hearing imprison (Marsiglia et al., 2018).

The idea of the program was to boost the morale and self-esteem of schoolchildren between LA public schools and the Los Angeles police departments. Resistance and temptation of drug use was the subject of the program. From 1983 to 1993, over a ten-year span, the police improved the program (Caputi & Thomas McLellan, 2017). The need for the program was understood and supported by the politicians, and they got involved in the pro-kids and pro-cops to make the strategy win-win. A tradition of administration was claimed to accomplish practical results through the implementation of DARE and celebrated on the National DARE Day (Thomas et al., 2015). All school districts accepted the program with the percentage of acceptance at 75 percent counted by DARE. The budget for the program was supported and applied by several government sources; meanwhile, millions were spent by each state for the raised affiliates (Flynn et al., 2015).

Researchers conducted extensive research on public health problems used to reduce the use of drugs. The behavioral use of the drug was altered to increase the effectiveness of the program and establish a wanted conclusion. The outcomes of the research indicated that there is no impact of the program on teens as there was no reduction in the use of drugs among children (Thomas et al., 2015). Similarly, the program limited the behaviors of adolescents to influence prevalence to reduce the use of drug programs. The implications of the program noted the adolescents have great support from the curricula about the use of drugs (Day et al., 2017).

Experiments were conducted regarding the use of alcohol and drugs. The adoption of persuading results was majored through opposing positions (Flynn, 2015). The investment made on DARE resulted in a decent return for the Justice Department. There was the significant difference between the students enrolled in the program and those not enrolled in the program (Caputi & Thomas McLellan, 2017).

The analysts directed extensive research on general wellbeing to confirm the achievement of the objectives such as the reduction of the utilization of medications. The utilization of medication was modified to expand the adequacy of the program. The results of the examination indicated there is no effect of the program on adolescents as there was no decrease in the utilization of medications among kids (Thomas et al., 2015). Fundamentally, it is differentiated that the program restricted the practices of youths to impact the notoriety; therefore, reducing the utilization of medication programs. The ramifications of the program noted the youths have extraordinary help from the educational program about the utilization of medications (Marsiglia et al., 2018).

The implementation of the program helped children resist the use of the drugs among the because of education (Thomas, McLellan, & Perera, 2015). Disciplines of the program own significant efficacy to ensure specific versions of improvements. Substantial reasons are considered to drive effective practices of the program and adapt evidence-based approaches to ensure decisions are supportive (Day et al., 2017).

Chapter Summary

The extent of drug-related crime is not evident, and it is probably impossible to state and determine the exact number of crimes, but the identification of drug related crime is significant by using several government sources and data accordingly. In the records of crime, it is found that victims found the offender in drugs influences less than the actual arrested criminal. It is also seen that crime is committed by the offender to get money for drugs. If adding all the crimes, causes, and influences on people, it is found that many of the criminal offenses are associated with drugs and a high number of the crimes are stated to be illegal possession. The occurrence of the crime is dependent on the structure of drug system to include transportation, manufacturing, production, and the sale of drugs.

The US statistics revealed that from 10 children, four are the victimizers of crimes related to drugs and among them; the percentage of drinkers is high. It is found that the drinkers use to drink alcohol for preceding offenses. The analysis on the use of substance indicated that negligence of parents towards children increases addiction and substance abuse and the percentage is expected to increase in the coming years.

The abuse problem or drug dependence was evident in 53 percent of the prisons and the outcomes of research conducted in 2004 revealed the state of potential improvement in the prisoners. The design of the program was associated to the target population, service resources and comprehension of the model in general terms, and included judicial interaction, assessment of needs, risks, responsivity, and offender screening, supervision and monitoring, incentives and graduated sanction, rehabilitation, and treatment services.

References

Allen, M. (2016). Police-reported crime statistics in Canada, 2015. Statistics Canada.

Bean, P. (2017). Drug courts, the judge, and the rehabilitative ideal. In Drug Courts (pp. 235-254). Routledge.

Bergen-Cico, D. K. (2015). War and drugs: The role of military conflict in the development of substance abuse. Routledge.

Brownstein, H. H. (2016). Drugs and violent crime. In The handbook of drugs and society (p. 371). John Wiley and Sons, Ltd West Sussex UK.

Caputi, T. L., & Thomas McLellan, A. (2017). Truth and DARE: Is DARE's new Keepin'it REAL curriculum suitable for American nationwide implementation?. Drugs: Education, Prevention and Policy, 24(1), 49-57.

Castañeda, J. G. (2018). Latin America and the End of the Cold War: an essay in frustration. In Latin America in a New World (pp. 28-52). Routledge.

Day, L. E., Miller-Day, M., Hecht, M. L., & Fehmie, D. (2017). Coming to the new DARE: A preliminary test of the officer-taught elementary keepin'it REAL curriculum. Addictive behaviors, 74, 67-73.

Engstrom, M., Wimberly, A., & Franke, N. (2017). Mass Incarceration: What's at Stake and What to Do.

Evans, W. N., Garthwaite, C., & Moore, T. J. (2018). Guns and Violence: The Enduring Impact of Crack Cocaine Markets on Young Black Males (No. w24819). National Bureau of Economic Research.

Flynn, A. B., Falco, M., & Hocini, S. (2015). Independent evaluation of middle school–based drug prevention curricula: a systematic review. JAMA pediatrics, 169(11), 1046-1052.

Foppe, K. S., Hammond-Weinberger, D. R., & Subedi, B. (2018). Estimation of the consumption of illicit drugs during special events in two communities in Western Kentucky, US using sewage epidemiology. Science of the Total Environment, 633, 249-256.

Fortner, M. J. (2016). Response to Daniel Kato's review of Black Silent Majority: The Rockefeller Drug Laws and the Politics of Punishment. Perspectives on Politics, 14(3), 834-835.

Gootenberg, P. (2015). Cocaine Powder and Crack Cocaine. The Handbook of Drugs and Society, 90.

Gossop, M. (2016). Living with drugs. Routledge.

Green, K. (2017). Black Silent Majority: The Rockefeller Drug Laws and the Politics of Punishment.

Greer, A. M., Martin, G., Joordens, C., & Macdonald, S. (2016). Motivations for Use of Crack Cocaine. In Neuropathology of Drug Addictions and Substance Misuse(pp. 229-236). Academic Press.

Guiney, C. (2016). The quality of crime statistics. Drugnet Ireland, 20-21.

Guney, E., Menche, J., Vidal, M., & Barábasi, A. L. (2016). Network-based in silico drug efficacy screening. Nature communications, 7, 10331.

Hari, J. (2015). Chasing the scream: The first and last days of the war on drugs. Bloomsbury Publishing US.

Harris, L. (2016). Black Silent Majority: The Rockefeller Drug Laws and the Politics of Punishment.

Hartung, D. M., Bourdette, D. N., Ahmed, S. M., & Whitham, R. H. (2015). The cost of multiple sclerosis drugs in the US and the pharmaceutical industry: too big to fail?. Neurology, 84(21), 2185-2192.

Huber III, A., Newman, R., & LaFave, D. (2016). Cannabis control and crime: Medicinal use, depenalization and the war on drugs. The BE Journal of Economic Analysis & Policy, 16(4).

Hueston, J., & Burke, K. (2016). Exporting Drug Court Concepts to Traditional Courts: A Roadmap to an Effective Therapeutic Court [Enter Paper Title]. Hueston, Jamey and Kevin Burke,

Exporting Drug Court Concepts to Traditional Courts: A Roadmap to an Effective Therapeutic Court,(2016) Court Review: Journal of the American Judges Association, 52(1).

Hutton, B., Salanti, G., Caldwell, D. M., Chaimani, A., Schmid, C. H., Cameron, C., ... & Mulrow, C. (2015). The PRISMA extension statement for reporting of systematic reviews incorporating network meta-analyses of health care interventions: checklist and explanations. Annals of internal medicine, 162(11), 777-784.

Kantor, E. D., Rehm, C. D., Haas, J. S., Chan, A. T., & Giovannucci, E. L. (2015). Trends in prescription drug use among adults in the United States from 1999-2012. Jama, 314(17), 1818-1830.

Lassiter, M. D. (2015). Impossible Criminals: The Suburban Imperatives of America's War on Drugs. Journal of American History, 102(1), 126-140.

Lim, Y. (2018). Understanding the War on Drugs in America through the Lens of Critical Race Theory. BLR, 156.

Maier, L., Pruteanu, M., Kuhn, M., Zeller, G., Telzerow, A., Anderson, E. E., ... & Patil, K. R. (2018). Extensive impact of non-antibiotic drugs on human gut bacteria. Nature, 555(7698), 623.

Malone, C. A. (2018). Beyond the Federal Drug War: A Panel Study of State-Level Powder and Crack Cocaine Laws, 1977–2010. Sociological Spectrum, 38(2), 117-144.

Marsiglia, F. F., Kulis, S. S., Kiehne, E., Ayers, S. L., Libisch Recalde, C. A., & Sulca, L. B. (2018). Adolescent substance-use prevention and legalization of marijuana in Uruguay: A feasibility trial of the keepin'it REAL prevention program. Journal of Substance use, 23(5), 457-465.

McColl, W. D. (2017). Theory and practice in the Baltimore city drug treatment court. In Drug Courts (pp. 3-26). Routledge.

Meier, K. J. (2016). The Politics of Sin: Drugs, Alcohol and Public Policy: Drugs, Alcohol and Public Policy. Routledge.

Miró, Ò., Dargan, P. I., Wood, D. M., Dines, A. M., Yates, C., Heyerdahl, F., ... & Galicia, M. (2019). Epidemiology, clinical features and management of patients presenting to European emergency departments with acute cocaine toxicity: comparison between powder cocaine and crack cocaine cases. Clinical Toxicology, 1-9.

Mott, M. M. (2018). Love the Prisoner, Ban the Substance: Pope Francis and the War on Drugs. In Pope Francis as a Global Actor (pp. 81-95). Palgrave Macmillan, Cham.

Murphy, J. (2015). Illness Or Deviance?: Drug Courts, Drug Treatment, and the Ambiguity of Addiction (p. 219). Philadelphia, PA: Temple University Press.

Nolan, J. (2017). Drug courts: In theory and in practice. Routledge.

Oliveira, H. P., Gonçalves, P. D., Ometto, M., Santos, B., Malbergier, A., Amaral, R., ... & Cunha, P. J. (2018). The route of administration exacerbates prefrontal functional impairments in crack cocaine users. Psychology of Addictive Behaviors, 32(7), 812.

Oteng-Ababio, M., Owusu, A. Y., Owusu, G., & Wrigley-Asante, C. (2017). Geographies of crime and collective efficacy in urban Ghana. Territory, Politics, Governance, 5(4), 459-477.

Palamar, J. J., Davies, S., Ompad, D. C., Cleland, C. M., & Weitzman, M. (2015). Powder cocaine and crack use in the United States: An examination of risk for arrest and socioeconomic disparities in use. Drug and alcohol dependence, 149, 108-116.

Pattillo, M. (2017). Black Silent Majority: The Rockefeller Drug Laws and the Politics of Punishment, by Michael Javen Fortner.

Peters, B. G. (2018). American public policy: Promise and performance. Cq Press.

Pettit, B., & Gutierrez, C. (2018). Mass Incarceration and Racial Inequality. American Journal of Economics and Sociology, 77(3-4), 1153-1182.

Redford, A., & Powell, B. (2016). Dynamics of Intervention in the War on Drugs: The Buildup to the Harrison Act of 1914. The Independent Review, 20(4), 509-530.

Ruiz, B., Ulibarrí, B. J., Lomelí, A. S., Guerra, R. S., & Longoria, R. R. (2018). The Relative Influence of Legal Pressure on Outcomes in a Rehabilitation Aftercare Drug Court. American Journal of Criminal Justice, 1-19.

Segal, B., Huba, G. J., & Singer, J. L. (2018). Drugs, daydreaming, and personality: A study of college youth. Routledge.

Shannon, E. (2015). Desperados: Latin drug lords, US lawmen, and the war America can't win. iUniverse.

Shimomura, E. T., Jackson, G. F., & Paul, B. D. (2019). Cocaine, Crack Cocaine, and Ethanol: A Deadly Mix. In Critical Issues in Alcohol and Drugs of Abuse Testing (pp. 215-224). Academic Press.

Spillane, J. F. (2016). Michael Javen Fortner. Black Silent Majority: The Rockefeller Drug Laws and the Politics of Punishment.

Temin, P. (2017). The Political Economy of Mass Incarceration: An Analytical Model.

Temin, P. (2018). The Political Economy of Mass Incarceration and Crime: An Analytic Model. International Journal of Political Economy, 1-13.

Thomas, R. E., McLellan, J., & Perera, R. (2015). Effectiveness of school-based smoking prevention curricula: systematic review and meta-analysis. BMJ open, 5(3), e006976.

Thomson, N. D. (2017). An exploratory study of female psychopathy and drug-related violent crime. Journal of interpersonal violence, 0886260517690876.

Villa, R. D., Rodrigues, T., & Bastos, F. C. (2016). South America in the Post-Cold War Era: war on drugs and the reshaping of the US security agenda. CAPA-REVISTA DA EGN, 21(1), 33-61.

Walker, M. A. (2015). Borders, one-dimensionality, and illusion in the war on drugs. Environment and Planning D: Society and Space, 33(1), 84-100.

CHAPTER EIGHT
COMMUNITY BASED CRIME CONTROL

Midtown Community Court (MCC)
History and Introduction

The New York criminal court consists of the Midtown Community Court (MCC) founded in 1993 in Time Square and focuses on crimes such as shoplifting, prostitution, quality of life offenses, vandalism, and farebeating to review the crimes and provide rehabilitation to avoid giving punishments (Beers, 2018). The judges could give several orders to the offenders, for instance, performing community service and other kinds of social services such as mental health counseling, drug treatments, and job training (Neal, 2015). The MCC is known as a collaboration of the Center for Court Innovation and New York State Unified Court System (Beers, 2018).

The foundation of the court depends on the residents, social service agencies, and business partnerships to organize projects that restitute communities and offer several on-site social services. In addition, the list of services includes job training for the community, mental health, and drug treatment (Jackson, 2018). The court is significantly different from other courts because

179

conventional courts assist the low-level offenders and combines help and punishment as a way to pay the community through services, whereas, the MCC addresses the people receiving social services as a way to gain underline a better understanding with criminal behavior (Mogulescu et al., 2016). The court rules from evaluation from the state courts and provides 75% of the community service needs of the city (Neal, 2015).

How Does It Work?

The purpose of the court is not to punish the offenders for their mistakes but focus on paying debts to society. In addition, the applications integrate into the rehabilitation of the offenders to serve the community at large, using reconciliation with the victims, indicating that the program focuses on the emergence of incarceration to reintegrate the skills and knowledge to pay back society (Mogulescu et al., 2016). The methods and topologies aimed to value the community at large with the assistance of the court system. Furthermore, the MCC is highly associated with offering restorative justice using financial counselors that play a significant role in the lives of children and brighten futures while, there is not a clear vision to interpret the meaning of this idea (Gruber et al., 2016).

The program is significantly associated with assisting people and ensuring the counseling and services are adequate to inspire people with empowerment and support to protect and employ resources with the capacity to stabilize economic condition

180

(Mogulescu et al., 2016). In addition, the resources are useful to offer a secure and peaceful environment to individuals. The issues of homelessness, financial inclusion, and reentry support are formalized to ensure the incardination of the program for the community and workforce development (Cohen, 2016). Typically, it is expected that the obstacles and struggle of people and families reduce with the implementation of the program as well as the rate of criminal histories would decrease to reduce crime (Mogulescu, Gruber, & Cohen, 2016).

There are certain areas focused by the program to enhance the justice system and contribute effectively to the strategies that support the community. The motivation behind the program include the causes and identification of criminal activities carried out in the city (Marks, 2017). The phenomenon also attempts to pay back the community to understand the needs of others thereby bringing peace and support to others. Through the MCC, designed activities and procedures provide punishments just for developing a bond between individuals to reduce the chances and occurrence of criminal activity in New York City (Mogulescu et al., 2016).

The establishment of the court is reliant on the nearby inhabitants, social administration offices and organizations to sort out ventures to restore networks and offer various on-location social administrations (Beers, 2018). The administrations incorporate the following elements such as work preparing for the network, psychological well-being advising, and medicate treatment for the general population. Ordinary courts help the low-level wrongdoers and combine help and discipline through the administration to better understand criminal conduct (Gruber et al., 2016).

This indicates the development of the court, the mechanisms, and changes that the court should bring into society, the rate of criminal activities, and the methods used to reduce crime. Through law enforcement offering advanced efforts for economic development, illegal activities are reduced by 24 percent and prostitution arrest decreased by 56 percent (Mogulescu et al., 2016).

Analysis of MCC

The primary purpose of the court is to bring community justice and support the idea with the adequate performance of the neighborhood of New York City as well as Harlem Brownsville, Red Hook, and others. In addition, the jurisdictional involvement of the whole world is considered for gaining interest and reduce the occurrence of incarceration using reinvigorating public trust (Jackson, 2018). The minor offending responses are included in the new forging. This launch of the community court grant program assists the justice system with the partnership of the Department of Justice Bureau of Justice Assistance in the US (Cohen, 2016).

The idea and need for assistance for the work align with community justice with improvements focused beyond the courts. In addition, some specific examples and applications are considered for encouraging the work of prosecutors under their norms and values to improve public trust, prevent crime, and offer justice to every individual (Gruber et al., 2016). The applications of the court connect to the sentences imposed in certain tallying cases and the effects of the court stem from the prosecutors for improving the attitudes of the community. Eventually, effort assists in improving criminal activities with the assistance of individual efforts made to engage the national experts and local prosecutors including the Fair & Just Prosecution and the Association of Prosecuting Attorneys. The court is the foundation of free assessment for the state courts and is meeting the consistency of 75 percent network administration need to help limit of the city (Marks, 2017).

Effectiveness of MCC and Evaluation

MCC is recognized as one of the key players in the reduction of drug use in the US and the popularization and spread of the system is associated with the drug court across the nation. NI stated 2600 courts are operating in the US that deal with drug activities (Beers, 2018). The activities of the court consist of concepts that combines actual consequences, real community, close judicial monitoring, and input from the community for developing the policy. The primary goal of using the technology designed indicates a sentencing decision for gathering broad information about the ongoing compliance monitoring process. Eventually, the model is essential for justifying intermediate sanctions with a broad range of choice offered to the judges (Mogulescu et al., 2016).

Criminal records are maintained to charge defendants. Criminal records were released through interviews to provide the defendant's information and placed into a database for downloading purposes (Neal, 2015). There are various tools included in the bottom right to expand the ability of geographical context to understand the record of arrested defendants. The statistical prediction allowed the alternative sanction for elaborating the chance of the defendant. The design offered technology aspects and information to the Ten Commandments of Electronic Court Design for presenting the ideas and organizing the results essential for the court (Gruber et al., 2016).

Gun Buy Back (GBB) Programs

Gun Buy Back Program Analysis

The implementation of the Gun Buy Back program in society was a positive step to give children knowledge about the elements causing problems in society. The chances of having a gun as a real toy in the future are high for children that use a gun as a toy in young age (Masters, 2016), and the implementation of the program could reduce the chances by giving children awareness. Children should understand the need for firearms and should respect the support offered to the community (Cook & Pollack, 2017).

The case revealed that it is difficult to imagine children with a gun playing in the bushes could cause gun usage thus programs could cause children to understand better playing methods causing the child turn away from toy guns (Hart, 2018). Safety is the most prominent factor and need of children that must be addressed in any situation to make the use of such toys a question (Jacobs, & Fuhr, 2017).

Taxpayers funded the gun buyback program and the cost of the program was hundreds of thousands of dollars to engage the anti-gun media to and improve conditions. The gun buyback program consisted of four interesting facts. The first fact was "bought back," the majority of the firearms are junk guns that are useless and no longer functioning (Cook & Pollack, 2017). The purpose was to indicate that the firearms were not used for crime related activities (Santaella-Tenorio et al. 2016).

The second fact was "no question asked," so the guns stolen were discovered in these activities and events, while, no one is allowed to ask questions about that indicating the possibility of stealing guns by the people that sold guns for money at the buybacks (Burley, 2018). If a criminal steals a gun and sells it to the government, the creation of such a program could leave everyone in danger. This will become a gun-running ring that can cause great harm and effect on the program (Santaella-Tenorio et al., 2016).

The third fact discovered from the program was "gun entrepreneurs," and offered a new market that means people are involved in the program to sell the guns for generating profit or gaining personal income (Cook & Pollack, 2017). In addition, the fourth fact was "come and find it," a fake reed for the government to find and defend rights through searching tons of accessories just for profit-making (Burley, 2018).

Gun Buy Back in New York

High attention is given to Gun Buyback Programs and is essential to rid guns used for evil on the streets. The functioning must not be a surprise for an individual and anti-gun community to indoctrinate kids to utilize these programs (Cook & Pollack, 2017). In addition, it is found that the program is focusing on the culture and programs associated with the ownership of a gun in New York. Fundamentally, the program is associated with the youth and encourages kids to bringing out their water pistols. Meanwhile, in the exchange of toy guns, new toys are given to the kids (Braga, 2017).

The purpose of doing these activities is to engage the youth at a young age to think that carrying guns and using guns as a toy is not good (Santaella-Tenorio et al., 2016). Using this strategy aided with teaching 2.5 million children per year that guns are bad because using guns is a disservice for the community. The program implemented in the lower middle schools as gun safety programs to understand, assist, and respect the use of firearms through the support of children (Green et al., 2017).

Evaluation and Analysis of GBB

The institution of the gun buyback program is associated with the private purchase of the owned firearms. The program aimed to reduce the number of civilians that bought firearms for criminal purposes. Civilians can sell these guns to local police (Fennelly & Perry, 2018). Different programs were initiated to control such activities and the participation for implementing the programs was anonymous and voluntary. The acceptance of legal and illegal weapons was formed and dependent on the programs. There were high units of ammunition estimated in the country; the outcomes of the program revealed that 104,782 firearms were collected with 747,000 ammunition units. The outcomes of the programs indicated that deaths, thefts, suicides, and accidents related to guns reduced (Baumann et al., 2017).

The citizens supported the program and the expenses of the program because of improving the conditions. The weapon buyback program comprised of four realities (Fennelly & Perry, 2018). A main actuality from the program was "repurchased," because this could include nonworking weapons. The weapons are given to remunerating the utilization of firearms is not authoritative and the reality was to show that the guns are not being used for wrongdoing (Ford, 2015).

It was mandatory that through the program, the police would destroy forearms and pay compensation. Changes in the policy was made after the firearms were in private hands. Finances for the program increased and changed the conditions of buyback programs for the state and territories (Baumann et al., 2017). Consistent regulations were introduced to improve the firearms laws and persons that participated were targeted for barrel

187

restrictions. The facts and policies were developed and agreed upon by the government. Overall, the policy ensured readily concealable and visually distinctive for the specialized and highly target pistols (Santaella-Tenorio et al., 2016).

The implementation of the program was monitored, and objectives were developed to endorse suggestive results. The regulations and implementation of the program resulted in stability and a reduction in the rate of the various problems in the community. Similar programs were carried out in the city determining effective results and minimizing the impact and penalties of crime (Cook & Pollack, 2017). The regulations strengthened legal activities and assisted with managing illegal terms to be imposed in New York. Violation of the program was monitored to ensure all the functioning and requirements focused on obtaining and accomplishing desirable objectives (Santaella-Tenorio et al., 2016).

Crime Victim Compensation in the US

Introduction

Crime Victim Compensation (CVC) is designed to assist victims with gaining financial costs given to the families for the cost of crime. The CVC program contains costs related to crime, like, medical treatment, counseling, loss of income, funerals, and other income factors that are not allowed to pay for many other sources (Malsch, 2017).

The goal of the program is to encourage the participation of victims in the prosecution and apprehension of criminals for the specific crime-related cost. Texas Legislature established the program in 1979, and the Attorney General managed the office. There are two types of compensation methods, crime victim's compensation and emergency medical care compensation (Moore & Milliner, 2017).

The program works for applying for compensation and awarding compensation to the victims of violent crimes. The programs require a review of the application by gathering information and ensuring that the candidate meets the eligibility criteria. In addition, the program verifies that a crime was reported and the occurrence of the crime is valid or not for reporting to law enforcement (Spalek, 2016). CVC is used to ask information from the applicant regarding the crime-related costs. The cost is paid by the staff to the applicant after reviewing the information in accordance with the rules of the program (Moore & Milliner, 2017).

Benefits

A government program that used for reimbursing the victims is known as crime victim compensation and the crime is associated with violent crimes. The list of crimes includes rape, homicide, assault, and burglary. In addition, the problems include the out-of-pocket expenses of families (Tennessee et al., 2017). State's across the globe have a crime victim compensation program. The program, crime victim compensation provides funds for counseling, dental and medical expenses, burial or funeral expenses, and support for lost wages (Garvin & Beloof, 2015).

Some of the states provide crime scene cleanup, financial counseling, court proceedings, medical treatment, or expenses for relocation for the victims if required for safety. In addition, the programs provide varies amounts for victim compensation based on the state varying from $10,000 to $100,000 (Johnston et al., 2018). Limitations on the expenses are applicable to certain expenses and includes burial expenses or funeral expenses on the amounts paid for medical expenses and counseling expenses (Garvin & Beloof, 2015). In order to receive funds there is the process of a claim, which occurs during the duration of a several weeks or months. Furthermore, in some states, this compensation is offered for a set period in terms of emergency awards and the compensation is categorized from $ 500 to $ 1000 and can include monies for emergency expenses like food, medications, or shelter (Johnston et al., 2018).

Eligibility

The criteria of eligibility are explained and categorized as follows.

Victims

The compensation must be given to the direct victim of a crime; however, only for violent crime. In some of the states, compensation is allotted only to the victims with physical injuries or traumatization from a violent crime (Elias, 2017).

Family Members

The families of homicide victims receive compensation for burial or funeral expenses, medical bills, and support counseling. The family members can also receive compensation for counseling in some cases, like child abuse, sexual assault, or domestic violence (Johnston et al., 2018). Meanwhile, there are specific requirements required to be addressed by the victim to get compensation beginning with the police that reports the crime stating the exceptions for children, reporting different times in the state, individual circumstances, and incapacitated victims (Garvin & Beloof, 2015).

The investigation includes cooperation with prosecutors and police for the prosecution of offenses; therefore, the state becomes applicable for the compensation. The victims submits an application for compensation, while exceptions occur for victims committing crimes such as drug dealing. Serious misconducts are involved in the contribution and causes of crime, which causes deaths or injuries. Crime and the cost of crime covered in the insurance for the programs like Workers' Compensation or Medicaid (Moore & Milliner, 2017).

191

Applications

To apply for crime victim compensation, victims or families must file a claim form in the state where the crime occurred. The compensation program then examines police records, receipts, and other information before deciding whether to pay a claim. For information about your state program, visit the National Association of Crime Victim Compensation Boards. The eligibility requirements of the applicants are investigated in order to receive compensation and there are guidelines and processes to receive the payment (Kunst et al., 2017).

CVC is used to retrieve data from the candidate concerning expenses from wrongdoing. The staff pay the cost to the candidate after an audit of the data on an agreement with the standards of the program (Johnston et al., 2018). The list of crimes where victims may receive compensation includes assault, ambush, theft, and assault in individual states. Furthermore, every state has a remuneration program based on violent crimes to help victims (Kunst et al., 2017). The program for injured individuals' remuneration pays for, directing costs, dental and restorative costs, entombment or burial service costs, and lost wages. In a portion of the states, the pay is dispensed just to the unfortunate casualties from got physical harm (Galvin et al., 2018).

Operation Ceasefire in Boston

Introduction

Operation Ceasefire recognized as the Boston Gun Project or the Boston Miracle. The problem orienting service of police realized in the year of 1996 in Boston was developed to help youth dealing with guns or violence. The primary purpose of this work based on the department of criminology (Ratcliffe et al., 2017). During the first era of the 1990s, cities like Boston in the US qualified and experienced a wide-range of youth, which is associated with the gun-homicide. The violence found stemmed mainly in poor inner cities (Tillyer et al., 2015). From studies, around 44% of the youth is associated with homicide. Operation ceasefire involved a problem-oriented service of police method and it is absorbed on the exact places where the crime occurred. Working of the interagency group composed of the following

- Analyses of qualitative research technique (Ratcliffe et al., 2016).
- Application of quantitative techniques of research.
- Evaluation of the impacts of involvements.
- Bent an assessment nature of the subtleties and dynamics for the violence of youth in Boston.
- Adaptation of the interference and involvement after implementation and sustained in the program (Ratcliffe et al., 2017).

- Operation ceasefire was mainly based upon the levers of pulling on the restricted strategies. Which emphasis the justice for the criminal enforcement on a less number of offenders and the youth, which are involved in gangs and responsible for the problems in the Boston.

- After the Operation Ceasefire, the number of youth homicides decreased (Henderson et al., 2017).

The Pareto Principle

An investigation conducted on Operation Ceasefire revealed that there is a strong connection between highly active criminals and severe violence. Violence increases with the increase of criminal groups and the collective involvement of groups that are associated at the city level to represent the population of offenders (Braga, 2017). The city population under 0.5% is connected to the population of victims, offenders, or both and underestimates lower bounds of the city and it is likely to state the incidents of street groups that are involved in the occurrence of the substantial portion. The population in Boston was about 556,180 people comprised of 61 separate groups and 1500 individuals identified. Roughly, 0.3% of the population of the city involved in homicides (Henderson et al., 2016).

The interventions conducted regarding the act of violence in the country aided with reducing the percentage of youth homicides. National Network for Safe Communities' was involved in this operation for identifying the intervention of violence. A robust empirical investigation was conducted for stating systematic review and concluding the collaboration of the review to state the effectiveness of crime prevention strategies (Henderson et al., 2017).

In some cities, gun homicide reduced by 42% because of Stockton's Operation Peacekeeper. Initiatives were taken for the project safe neighborhoods to reduce the overall percentage of homicides at a mass level. Great efforts were made for gun assault reduction and records indicated a reduction in violence and homicide association (Ratcliffe et al., 2016).

Results and Impacts

The National Network provided information about the operation ceasefire for Safe Communities known as a violence reduction strategy through John Jay College of Criminal Justice (Henderson et al., 2016). Information about the practitioner's tools and advanced implementation materials, along with the underlying factors, was provided. In particular, it presented the main components of the strategy and provided a briefing about the highlighted areas of the report for the case (Ratcliffe et al., 2016).

The ceasefire investigation was perceived as the Boston Gun Project or the Boston Marvel and is characterized as the issue by the administration of police in 1996 in Boston. On a substantial scale, the program was implied for youth weapons quality or viciousness (Ratcliffe et al., 2017). The primary reason for this work depends on the division of criminology. Over in the underlying period of the 1990s, numerous urban communities like Boston qualified and experienced a wide range of youth related to the firearm crime (Tillyer et al., 2015). Brutality was primarily engaged in internal poor urban areas. From the ongoing examinations, 44 percent of adolescent is related to the crime. Task truce included an issue-situated administration of police technique and assimilated on the accurate spots where the wrongdoing occurred (Henderson et al., 2016).

There was a significant statistical decrease in the number of youth homicides monthly in Boston due to the implementation of the operation applied at mass level in the ceasefire. Notably, there was a reduction of 63 percent in the number of victims, however, it is suggesting the average percentage on a monthly basis was 3.5 and the outcomes of the posttest mean indicated that the percentage of youth homicides in a month was 1.3 (Ratcliffe et al., 2016). There were certain variables applied to control the trends and includes employment rates and violence trends in the city. The models of data analysis presented the elements to influence reduction and causes for substantive change in the intervention associated with the Ceasefire and youth homicides (Tillyer et al., 2015).

The guideline drafted a decrease in the rate and tasks of youth crime as far as the mediations led concerning the demonstration of viciousness in the nation. The National Network for Safe Communities' engaged with this activity to distinguish the mediation of viciousness. The robust experimental examination was directed for expressing precise audits and closing the cooperation of the survey to express the adequacy of wrongdoing avoidance techniques (Ratcliffe et al., 2017).

Similarly, the reduction in gun assault was evident from the investigation and implementation of the principles and the 25% decrease in the gun assaults was seen in the district D-2; however, the reductions did not occur based on the data obtained from the principles of the programs (Tillyer et al., 2015). Interventions of Ceasefire were also associated with the shots-fired calls for service citywide, the percentage reduction was 32 as found on monthly analysis and there was little impact of the applied policy in the reduction. In addition, the recovery of crime ratio was evident and kept the lowest level for reflecting a steady reduction in crime from time-to-time (Tillyer et al., 2015).

Chapter Summary

The New York criminal court consists of Midtown Community Court, which focuses on shoplifting, prostitution, quality of life offenses, vandalism, and farebeating to ensure the phenomenon and application of rehabilitation to avoid giving punishments. The judges could give several orders to the offenders, for instance, performing a community service activity and kinds of social service like mental health counseling, drug treatment, and job training. The court was founded in the year 1993 in New York in Time Square as the MCC and is as a collaboration of the Center for Court Innovation and New York State Unified Court System.

The implementation of the Gun Buy Back Program in society is a positive step to give children knowledge about the consequences of bad behavior. The chances of owning a real gun in the future are high for the children that use a gun as a toy at a young age. In addition, the implementation of the program helps with awareness and children must understand the need for firearms.

The program that is designed to assist the victims with financial cost because of crime is the CVC program and covers expenses such as medical treatment, counseling, loss of income, funerals, and other income factors. The goal of the program is to encourage reimbursing victims and punishing criminals for the specific crime-related cost for the innocent victims. Texas Legislature established the program in 1979 and the Attorney General managed the office. There are two types of compensation methods crime victim compensation and emergency medical care compensation.

References

Baumann, L., Clinton, H., Berntsson, R., Williams, S. S., Rovella, J. C., Shapiro, D., ... & Campbell, B. T. (2017). Suicide, guns, and buyback programs: An epidemiologic analysis of firearm-related deaths in Connecticut. *Journal of trauma and acute care surgery*, *83*(6), 1195-1199.

Beers, J. A. (2018). *Courage: A Ministry of Hope*. Dog Ear Publishing.

Braga, A. A. (2017). Long-term trends in the sources of Boston crime guns. *RSF: The Russell Sage Foundation Journal of the Social Sciences*, *3*(5), 76-95.

Braga, A. A. (2017). Long-term trends in the sources of Boston crime guns. *RSF: The Russell Sage Foundation Journal of the Social Sciences*, *3*(5), 76-95.

Burley, D. (2018). The Ban down under: United States Should Adopt Australian-Style Gun Regulations to Curb Rising Rate of Elderly Suicides. *Elder LJ*, *26*, 149.

Cohen, A. J. (2016). Trauma and the welfare state: a genealogy of prostitution courts in New York city. *Tex. L. Rev.*, *95*, 915.

Cook, P. J., & Pollack, H. A. (2017). Reducing access to guns by violent offenders. *RSF: The Russell Sage Foundation Journal of the Social Sciences*, *3*(5), 2-36.

Elias, R. (2017). *Victims of the System*. Routledge.

Fennelly, L. J., & Perry, M. A. (2018). Crime and Effective Community Crime Prevention Strategies. In *CPTED and Traditional Security Countermeasures* (pp. 364-366). CRC Press.

Ford, T. L. (2015). Gun Buy-Backs: A Proposed New Strategy. *The McNair Scholarly Review*, 45.

Galvin, M. A., Loughran, T. A., Simpson, S. S., & Cohen, M. A. (2018). Victim compensation policy and white-collar crime: Public preferences in a national willingness-to-pay survey. *Criminology & Public Policy*, *17*(3), 553-594.

Garvin, M., & Beloof, D. E. (2015). Crime victim agency: Independent lawyers for sexual assault victims. *Ohio St. J. Crim. L.*, *13*, 67.

Green, J., Damle, R. N., Kasper, R. E., Violano, P., Manno, M., Nazarey, P. P., ... & Hirsh, M. P. (2017). Are "goods for guns" good for the community? An update of a community gun buyback program. *Journal of trauma and acute care surgery*, *83*(2), 284-288.

Gruber, A., Cohen, A. J., & Mogulescu, K. (2016). Penal welfare and the new human trafficking intervention courts. *Fla. L. Rev.*, *68*, 1333.

Hart, F. (2018). Gun Control–Outreach vs Legislation.

Henderson, S. M., Peterson, S. S., & Engel, R. S. (2016). Pulling Levers to Prevent Violence:"The Boston Miracle," Its. *Preventing Crime and Violence*, 281.

Henderson, S. M., Peterson, S. S., & Engel, R. S. (2017). Pulling Levers to Prevent Violence:"The Boston Miracle," Its Adaptations, and Future Directions for Research. In *Preventing Crime and Violence* (pp. 281-296). Springer, Cham.

Jackson, A. (2018). Addressing the criminalization of survivors of sex trafficking: Recommendations for judicial and legislative improvement.

Jacobs, J. B., & Fuhr, Z. (2017). The Potential and Limitations of Universal Background Checking for Gun Purchasers. *Wake Forest JL & Pol'y, 7*, 537.

Johnston, D. W., Shields, M. A., & Suziedelyte, A. (2018). Victimisation, Well-being and Compensation: Using Panel Data to Estimate the Costs of Violent Crime. *The Economic Journal, 128*(611), 1545-1569.

Kunst, M. J. J., Koster, N. N., & Van Heugten, J. (2017). Performance evaluations and victim satisfaction with state compensation for violent crime: A prospective study. *Journal of interpersonal violence, 32*(19), 3027-3044.

Malsch, M. (2017). *Crime, victims and justice: essays on principles and practice*. Routledge.

Marks, L. K. (2017). The Unified Court System's Response to the Opioid Epidemic in New York. *Alb. Gov't L. Rev., 11*, 28.

Masters, J. (2016). US gun policy: global comparisons. *Council on Foreign Relations*.

Mogulescu, K., Gruber, A., & Cohen, A. J. (2016). Penal Welfare and the New Human Trafficking Intervention Courts.

Moore, L., & Milliner, B. (2017). Legal supports for trafficked persons: Assisting survivors via certification, state/federal benefits, and compensation. In *Human Trafficking Is a Public Health Issue* (pp. 251-262). Springer, Cham.

Neal, A. (2015). Homosexuality in the Heartland: Alternative Print Media from 1970s Kansas City.

Ratcliffe, J. H., Perenzin, A., & Sorg, E. T. (2016). Operation Thumbs Down.

Ratcliffe, J. H., Perenzin, A., & Sorg, E. T. (2017). Operation Thumbs Down: A quasi-experimental evaluation of an FBI gang takedown in South Central Los Angeles. *Policing: An International Journal of Police Strategies & Management, 40*(2), 442-458.

Santaella-Tenorio, J., Cerdá, M., Villaveces, A., & Galea, S. (2016). What do we know about the association between firearm legislation and firearm-related injuries?. *Epidemiologic reviews, 38*(1), 140-157.

Spalek, B. (2016). *Crime victims: Theory, policy and practice.* Macmillan International Higher Education.

Tennessee, A. M., Bradham, T. S., White, B. M., & Simpson, K. N. (2017). The monetary cost of sexual assault to privately insured US women in 2013. *American journal of public health, 107*(6), 983-988.

Tillyer, M. S., Engel, R. S., & Lovins, B. (2015). Beyond Boston. *Critical Issues in Policing: Contemporary Readings*, 401.

CHAPTER NINE
LEGITIMACY AND COMPLIANCE AND INSANITY DEFENSE

Introduction

The possibility of finishing government form stems from the view of deliberate consistency. In any case, it is connected to the method for asserting decreases and announcing a person's salary. There are rules provided that should have been pursued. The assessment code depends on the desires of IRS citizens to plan various rules. Data gathered on the correct filling status of a citizen uncovered whether the individual is qualifying or reliant. The law wards off people from committing crimes because of individual fulfillment and the results of encroaching upon the law usually fits the lousy behavior (Patterson, 2018). Many cases result in prolonged or brief confinement where the length of the sentence reflects the illicit conduct or unlawful movement to keep other potential culprits from attempting the same bad behavior. Individuals review the jobs of the police to feel secure and exercise their human rights with hopes to decrease wrongdoing (Dolovich & Natapoff, 2017). Adequacy and security for the public comes with the job of the police. People inside dealt with social affairs consistently conceal their feelings of responsibility to comply with the guidelines of the group. Group members trust specialists feel that the guidelines of group specialists are genuine, and fit the bill (Schmalleger, 2017).

Voluntary Compliance

The principles of taxpayers are referred to as voluntary compliance and used to enhance the tax system using accurate annual returns and honest corporate filings. The income tax system of the US operates under the considerate assumptions of the tax system. (Cole et al., 2018). Taxpayers has to complete the IRS to get a return on paid tax. The idea of completion of a tax return is associated with the perception of voluntary compliance and is applied in the way of claiming reductions and reporting individual income (Dolovich & Natapoff, 2017). There are guidelines provided that should be followed and the tax code is based on the expectations of IRS taxpayers to schedule numerous guidelines. Credits or deductions are associated with the items of taxpayers when qualified. Information collected on the right filling status of taxpayer reveals whether the person is qualifying or is dependent (Schmalleger, 2017).

The obligations of income tax are estimated to file the status of return and withholdings for the money owed by an individual. Taxpayers are required to fill out a tax return during tax time for adherence to voluntary compliance. There is extra income required for part-time work of the taxpayer entity must be followed to meet the requirements (Pound, 2018). It makes forms for taxpayers effective to send information and other reports of income and the taxpayer must pay attention to the compilation with the regulations of the IRS to develop tax returns and report income (Neubauer & Fradella, 2018). The reports of the income are decided for taxpayers and the IRS is needed to recalculate and audit the tax return obligations of income tax (Patterson, 2018).

Why Do People Obey the Law?

In general, the purpose of the law is to protect, ensure rights, maintain order, and reduce the intensity of crime in particular. The formalization of law gives the direction of what is correct and incorrect to an individual and without laws, there will be no justice in the community. In addition, the purpose of obeying the law is to ensure the security of rights (Neubauer & Fradella, 2018). Law is responsible for a secondary role in social behavior by implementing direct rules on society. No one is perfect and everybody in society can break the rules sometimes intentionally and sometimes non-intentionally with individuals intentionally not paying taxes (Lamont, 2016).

Furthermore, the young generation is drowning under the darkness of drugs and illegal practice of sex. People need to obey the law to protect themselves from the conflicts of right and wrong (Terrill et al., 2016). Law helps to keep away

205

individuals that adversely influences the personal satisfaction of other individuals and the outcomes of infringing upon the law regularly fits the wrongdoing. For example, influencing someone to complete activities that cause minor damage (Kaiser & Holtfreter, 2016). Different cases result in prolonged or brief detainment where the length of the term mirrors the seriousness of the illegal behavior or unlawful activity to prevent other potential lawbreakers from similar wrongdoing.

Moreover, social rules and regulations are made by society members (Terrill et al., 2016). If someone does not obey the law, punishment may occur. There are adequate laws developed by authorities of every country, and these laws ensure the security and safety of everyone (Beijersbergen et al., 2016).

Law is not simple and deals with wicked people in order to stop criminal activity. There are circumstances where if everybody seeks after their very own personal responsibility, everybody will be more appalling off than they would have been if they acted unexpectedly (Kaiser & Holtfreter, 2016). This is the turnaround of the 'undetectable hand' where if everybody seeks after their circumstance, everybody in the network is improved of, as though everybody's activities are guided by an 'imperceptible hand' to accomplish a goal (Beijersbergen et al., 2016). In this regard, a network of self-intrigued performing artists needs law:

- To settle 'Detainee's quandary' circumstances.

- To convey into private hands property that would make everybody abuse some way or another, subsequently maintaining a strategic distance from a 'disaster of the center's circumstance emerging (Bradford et al., 2015).

- To forestall individuals following up on their normal need to remove 'tit for tat' in vengeance or saw wrongs that they have endured at other individuals' hands (Kaiser & Holtfreter, 2016).

What Do People Want from The Police?

A group of people whose job is to uphold government rules and regulations and make the ordinary people pay attention to the rules are police. Police have the duty to help people in emergencies such as saving their property and lives, and protecting them from criminal acts (Tankebe et al., 2016). Furthermore, members of the police force are trained to give first aid to people in emergencies because they are the first on the scene. Police help to prevent crime and protect the common public (Murphy et al., 2016). People want an immediate response from the police when reporting a crime and police officers should arrive quickly. Uniformed cops are appointed to watch specific geographic regions, which they check for indications of crime. Officers likewise direct ventures and arrest guilty parties (Nagin & Telep, 2017). Officers complete specific tasks based on experience and may work using bicycles, use canines, ride horses, or drive cruisers (Tankebe et al., 2016). In addition, studies have revealed that people are focusing on the role of police at large, the basic need of people is to protect and assist in attaining legal rights and the people expect a reduction in the rate of crime. Effectiveness and security in society have resulted in the role police play in society (Beijersbergen et al., 2016).

The Psychology of Legitimacy

Individuals inside sorted out gatherings regularly cover up their sentiments of commitment to obey the rules. Individuals trust only team experts and feel that the standards of team experts are real and subsequently, qualified for being compiled (Nagin & Telep, 2017). Team individuals deliberately acknowledge and obey choices from gathering specialists. Research draws on proof from investigations of experts in political, lawful, administrative, instructive, and family settings that investigated why individuals see as real and willfully concede to bunch specialists (Murphy et al., 2016). Two speculations about authenticity include asset-based hypotheses, spoken to by instrumental models, and distinguishing proof-based speculations, spoken to by the social model. The discoveries give substantial help to the presence of a social segment of authenticity, proposing that specialists draw a vital piece of their authenticity from their social associations with gathering individuals. The discoveries additionally demonstrate that there is an instrumental part of authenticity (Tankebe et al., 2016).

Consequently, the brain science of authenticity includes both instrumental and social components. Investigation mishaps are another essential duty, which is a visible part of the responsibilities of police officers. Officers may coordinate traffic, review the scene, observe on any single activity of the society, give medical aid to any harmed human, and take composed proclamations from drivers. Other fundamental undertakings incorporate clearing any destruction and coordinating or rerouting traffic (Beijersbergen et al., 2016).

Insanity Defense

What Is the Insanity Defense?

The mental disorder defense is known as the insanity defense and it is used for the evaluation of criminal case with the affirmation of defense argues responsibility and actions of the defendant for becoming persistent or episodic psychiatric diseases that are associated to the criminal acts at the time. The actions are contrasted with provocation excuse to decrease defendant responsibility (Rogers, 2015). The findings of the criminal trial stand for finding contrast in the defendant case and the prevention of mental diseases for assisting and counseling. Besides, a mental disorder prevents individuals from estates, trusts, and civil findings (Alden, 2018). The civil commitments are considered for an individual to reveal the mental institution of the disabled. The full criminal punishment is exempted based on the code of Hammurabi on traditional grounds (Rogers, 2015), reflecting capital commissions for informing lack of provisions and code rule for various mental disorders. In criminal law, statutory legislations are formalized to understand the reasons for the mental disorder to use the mental illness as a defense (Reid, 2015).

The forensic mental health professionals evaluate the jurisdictions for making the guides appropriate to allow the accusations of criminals. The mental health practitioners understand the responsibility for deciding the matters of criminal responsibility utilizing the jury (White, 2017). Besides, the defendants are elaborating the last issues to make restrained judgments about health practitioners and some jurisdictions are using a mental illness for the defense during the plea. The commitments are followed for an indefinite period for dealing with the psychiatric facility (Cox, 2017).

Insanity Defense Reform Act Of 1984

The Insanity Defense Reform Act, this law signed in October 1984 as the first comprehensive federal legislation on the topic. The deposition of the law is considered for people suffering from mental diseases; meanwhile, the individuals involved in the criminal justice system (Moriarty, 2016). The provisions of the act are as follows:

- To establish defense placed to proof burden on the defendant by convincing and unequivocal evidence.

- Expert testimony scope was limited on decisive legal problems

- Elimination of diminished capacity on the defense (Cox, 2017).

- The statement "not guilty only by reason of insanity," was developed for dealing with a special verdict that has the capacity of triggering proceeding of commitment.

- The person became insane in the condition of having the feeling of guilty provided to federal commitment, or the person serves the federal prison sentence (White, 2017).

President Ronald Reagan signed it into law for defending and governing the defendants using insanity reasons. The component of volitional was removed regarding a lack of the defendant to conform to the capacity of law using the test. Exculpation of the defendant was acceptable in the result of a defect or severe mental issues (Moriarty, 2016).

However, the appreciation of quality and nature was not focused on identifying the acts of wrongfulness although creating the law stemmed from public outrage. The government considered the standards of insanity before implementing the enactment of the law (Collins, 2018). The insanity plea allowed reasonable doubt regarding the defendant's insanity proof. However, the assumptions listed were analyzed to state if the person is legally insane. Constitutions were implemented to check the health and capacities of the individual and the rational of the mental condition was attacked to criticize ineffective judgments (Smith, 2017).

Durham vs. United State Case Analysis

Durham v. the United States, 214 F.2d 862 (D.C. Cir. 1954) is a criminal case. Durham rules associated with a defendant who was not found guilty in front of the jury because the findings of the case revealed that if a person is going through mental health issues, he or she is not responsible any unlawful or criminal acts (Moriarty, 2016). Furthermore, in the case, the psychiatrists were playing a role to inform the character and mental disease of the defendant to the jury. In this regard, the jury could understand the disease of the defendant using the information provided to understand the defendant's situation (Smith, 2018).

It was required to elaborate on the determinations of the juries to analyze and state the expert testimony on the disease. In addition, the State v. Pike followed findings of the case and this implementation of the case instructions were not helpful. The instructions and suggestions of the case were adopted and followed in two states to influence and continue the legal debate over insanity (Lacroix et al., 2017). High criticism was faced by the jury faced high criticism when deciding the case and there was no standard of control or reason for the impairment made by the judge. Meanwhile, the investigation of the case showcased no definition of mental disease and in the end, the jury was left to decide based on the instructions of expert testimony (Perlin, 2016).

M'Naghten Test

The rule for finding and analyzing criminal insanity is M'Naghten rule. Defendants use the rule when not guilty for criminal activities because of insanity. The case highlighted the investigation about alleged criminal activity at a time when the defendant does not understand the impact of the quality and nature of those actions (Buder, 2018). Daniel M'Naghten was found deranged while conducting poor actions in the case of attempting to kill a Prime Minister (Farrell, 2016). An attempt occurred to shot and kill Peel and M'Naghten thought he wanted to kill him so M'Naghten killed Peel's secretary. The medical experts conducted an investigation and found that M'Naghten was psychotic, and for that, he is not guilty (Buder, 2018).

The verdict was analyzed based on the definitions of criminal insanity, after the investigation, Lords of Justice considered all the elements and compiled the information to determine innocence under the reason of defect due to the disease of the mind. The quality and nature of doing an act is the factor that can state that the action is wrong or not (Weiss & Gupta, 2018).

The development of the M'Naghten Test rule was formalized to limit insanity. Inability was the essential component to distinguish the actions of right from wrong, which is stated as a defense to cognitive insanity. The formulation of other tests informed insanity as volitional insanity by the courts and legislatures (Farrell, 2016). The persons that have mental instability could performs a criminal act without distinguishing right from wrong; however, the criminal acts and volitional insanity was rejected by many of the jurisdictions and legislatures (Weiss & Gupta, 2018).

Insanity Defense and Burden of Proof

In the legal defense system, insanity is a legal action and is also considered as a shield of mental illness that criminals used to protect and brunt the legal system. In addition, the criminal justice system has high claims and concerns about the manipulation of laws due to mental illness (Smith, 2018). The courts struggled to construct a balance for protecting the system from the abuse of mental illness and protect individuals that have the capacity to abuse the system. In this regard, colossal research and investigations analyzed and discussed activities of the insanity defense, while, the courts required various requirements for elaborating and justifying the claim of insanity by the defendant (Corrado, 2017).

The term burden of proof is a question for the insanity defense associated with the essential sources of controversy. Before the Hinckley verdict burden of proof was considered as a place for the majority of states in which the prosecutor was required to prove non-insanity of the defendant (Robinson & Williams, 2017). However, after the case, a defense was required to prove the insanity of the defendant. Meanwhile, the burden of proving the insanity of defense was on the shoulders of states and it was essential for the defense to reflect either by convincing through unequivocal evidence of insanity. In addition, it is still a burden for the prosecutors to prove the insanity of the defendant beyond all the proved, considerate, and reasonable doubts (Smith, 2018).

Chapter Summary

The mental disorder defense is known as insanity defense and is used for the evaluation of criminal cases with the affirmation of defense argues responsibility and actions of the defendant for becoming persistent or episodic psychiatric diseases that are associated to the criminal acts. The actions are contrasted with provocation to decrease responsibility to the state defendant responsibility. The forensic mental health professionals are evaluating the jurisdictions for making the guides appropriate to allow accusations with criminal responsibilities interconnected and testimony guides. The mental health practitioners understand the responsibility for deciding the matters of criminal responsibility using the jury. President Ronald Reagan signed it into law for defending and governing the defendants contain insanity reasons. The component of volitional was removed regarding lack of the defendant to conform to the capacity of law using the test. Exculpation of the defendant was acceptable in the condition of time of commission to consult the acts of offense in the result of a defect or severe mental issues. When the jury decided on the case, they faced high criticism and there was no standard of control or reason for the impairment made by the judge.

Meanwhile, it is indicated by the investigation of the case that there was not any particular definition of mental disease. In the end, the jury was left to decide on the instructions of expert testimony. The development of the M'Naghten Test rule was formalized to limit insanity. Inability was the essential component to distinguish the actions right from wrong, which is stated as a defense to cognitive insanity. The formulation of other tests informed insanity as volitional insanity by the courts and legislatures. It is expected from the persons that have mental instability that perform a criminal act without distinguishing right from wrong. However, the criminal acts and volitional insanity was rejected by many of the jurisdictions and legislatures.

References

Alden, A. L. (2018). Disorder in the Court: Morality, Myth, and the Insanity Defense. University of Alabama Press.

Beijersbergen, K. A., Dirkzwager, A. J., & Nieuwbeerta, P. (2016). Reoffending after release: Does procedural justice during imprisonment matter?. Criminal Justice and Behavior, 43(1), 63-82.

Bradford, B., Hohl, K., Jackson, J., & MacQueen, S. (2015). Obeying the rules of the road: Procedural justice, social identity, and normative compliance. Journal of contemporary criminal justice, 31(2), 171-191.

Buder, S. (2018, May). Failures of the M'Naghten Rules: Women and the Insanity Defence in Victorian England. In Inquiry@ Queen's Undergraduate Research Conference Proceedings.

Cole, G. F., Smith, C. E., & DeJong, C. (2018). The American system of criminal justice. Cengage Learning.

Collins, E. (2018). Insane: James Holmes, Clark V. Arizona, and America's Insanity Defense. JL & Health, 31, 33.

Corrado, M. L. (2017). Punishment and the Burden of Proof.

Cox, K. I. (2017). The Need for Reform: A Comprehensive Legislative Analysis of the Illinois Slayer Statute. Charleston L. Rev., 11, 119.

Dolovich, S., & Natapoff, A. (Eds.). (2017). The New Criminal Justice Thinking. NYU Press.

Farrell, P. T. (2016). A Judge Views the M'Naghten Rule. The Catholic Lawyer, 4(4), 4.

Kaiser, K. A., & Holtfreter, K. (2016). An integrated theory of specialized court programs: Using procedural justice and therapeutic jurisprudence to promote offender compliance and rehabilitation. Criminal Justice and Behavior, 43(1), 45-62.

Kaiser, K. A., & Holtfreter, K. (2016). An integrated theory of specialized court programs: Using procedural justice and therapeutic jurisprudence to promote offender compliance and rehabilitation. Criminal Justice and Behavior, 43(1), 45-62.

Lacroix, R., O'Shaughnessy, R., McNiel, D. E., & Binder, R. L. (2017). Controversies concerning the Canadian not criminally responsible reform act. Journal of the American Academy of Psychiatry and the Law, 45(1), 44-51.

Lamont, C. K. (2016). International criminal justice and the politics of compliance. Routledge.

Moriarty, J. C. (2016). Seeing Voices: Potential Neuroscience Contributions to a Reconstruction of Legal Insanity. Fordham L. Rev., 85, 599.

Murphy, K., Bradford, B., & Jackson, J. (2016). Motivating compliance behavior among offenders: Procedural justice or deterrence?. Criminal Justice and Behavior, 43(1), 102-118.

Nagin, D. S., & Telep, C. W. (2017). Procedural justice and legal compliance. Annual Review of Law and Social Science, 13, 5-28.

Neubauer, D. W., & Fradella, H. F. (2018). America's courts and the criminal justice system. Cengage Learning.

Patterson, G. T. (2018). Introduction to Evidence-Based Practices and Principles in the Criminal Justice System. Clinical Interventions in Criminal Justice Settings: Evidence-Based Practice, 1.

Perlin, M. L. (2016). The insanity defense: Nine myths that will not go away. The Insanity Defense: Multidisciplinary Views on Its History, Trends, and Controversies (Mark D. White, Editor.

Pound, R. (2018). Criminal justice in America. Routledge.

Reid, B. (2015). Incompetency and Insanity: Public Policy Issues Are Inadequately Addressed. Ethics & Critical Thinking Journal, 2015(3).

Robinson, P. H., & Williams, T. (2017). MAPPING AMERICAN CRIMINAL LAW Variations Across the Fifty States: Ch. 14 Insanity Defense.

Rogers, R. (2015). 5 An Introduction to Insanity Evaluations. Learning Forensic Assessment: Research and Practice, 97.

Schmalleger, F. (2017). Criminal justice. Pearson.

Smith, J. R. (2017). Invested with a Strange Authority: A Guide to the Insanity Defense and Related Issues in Tennessee. Lincoln Mem'l UL Rev., 5, 20.

Smith, J. R. (2018). Invested With a Strange Authority: A Guide to the Insanity Defense and Related Issues in Tennessee. Lincoln Memorial University Law Review, 5(2), 2.

Smith, J. R. (2018). Invested With a Strange Authority: A Guide to the Insanity Defense and Related Issues in Tennessee. Lincoln Memorial University Law Review, 5(2), 2.

Tankebe, J., Reisig, M. D., & Wang, X. (2016). A multidimensional model of police legitimacy: A cross-cultural assessment. Law and Human Behavior, 40(1), 11.

Terrill, W., Paoline III, E. A., & Gau, J. M. (2016). Three pillars of police legitimacy: Procedural justice, use of force, and occupational culture. In The politics of policing: between force and legitimacy (pp. 59-76). Emerald Group Publishing Limited.

Weiss, K. J., & Gupta, N. (2018). America's First M'Naghten Defense and the Origin of the Black Rage Syndrome. The journal of the American Academy of Psychiatry and the Law, 46(4), 503-512.

White, M. D. (Ed.). (2017). The Insanity Defense: Multidisciplinary Views on Its History, Trends, and Controversies. ABC-CLIO.

Made in the USA
Middletown, DE
08 August 2020

14790270R00132